THE MASTER'S WAY
OF PERSONAL EVANGELISM

OTHER BOOKS BY ROBERT E. COLEMAN

The Coming World Revival

Established by the Word

Introducing the Prayer Cell

Life in the Living Word

The Master Plan of Evangelism

The Spirit and the Word

Dry Bones Can Live Again

One Divine Moment (Editor)

Written in Blood

Evangelism in Perspective

They Meet the Master

Songs of Heaven

Growing in the Word

The New Covenant

The Heartbeat of Evangelism

Evangelism on the Cutting Edge (Editor)

The Master Plan of Discipleship

Nothing to Do but to Save Souls

The Great Commission Lifestyle

THE MASTER'S WAY
OF PERSONAL EVANGELISM

Robert E. Coleman

CROSSWAY BOOKS • WHEATON, ILLINOIS
A DIVISION OF GOOD NEWS PUBLISHERS

The Master's Way of Personal Evangelism

Copyright © 1997 by Robert E. Coleman

Published by Crossway Books
    a division of Good News Publishers
    1300 Crescent Street
    Wheaton, Illinois 60187

Cover Design: D² DesignWorks

Cover Illustration: *Christ and the Woman of Samaria* by Anton Dorph
                  (Superstock)

First printing, 1997

Printed in the United States of America

Scripture quotations are taken from the *New American Standard Bible* ®
© Copyright The Lockman Foundation 1960, 1962, 1963, 1968, 1971, 1972, 1973, 1975, 1977. Used by permission.

Library of Congress Cataloging-in-Publication Data
Coleman, Robert Emerson, 1928-
    The Master's way of personal evangelism / Robert E. Coleman.
       p.   cm.
    Includes bibliographical references.
    ISBN 0-89107-912-2 (alk. paper)
    1. Jesus Christ—Evangelistic methods.   2. Evangelistic work.
  I. Title.
    BT590.E8C64   1997
    269'.2—dc20   96-41251

05		04		03		02		01		00		99		98		97
15	14	13	12	11	10	9	8	7	6	5	4	3	2	1

In memory of
Sollie and Lilla McCreless—
loving servants of Christ
whose vision and support of evangelism
have enlarged the ministries
of countless students around the world.

CONTENTS

INTRODUCTION

What Is Evangelism?

An artist once sought to depict on canvas the meaning of evangelism. He painted a picture of a storm at sea. Black tempestuous clouds filled the sky with forewarnings of disaster. Illumined by a flash of lightning, a little boat dashed against the breakers in the raging waves. The stricken vessel was disintegrating under the pounding of the ocean. Sailors struggled in the swirling waters, their anguished voices crying out for help. But there was no help.

The only glimmer of hope could be seen in the foreground where a large rock protruded out of the sea. And there, clutching desperately with both hands, was one lone seaman.

It was a moving scene. Looking at the painting, one could see in the tempest a symbol of mankind's hopeless condition. And, true to the Scripture, the only way of salvation was the

Rock of Ages, a shelter in the time of storm. But as the artist reflected upon his work, he realized that he had not accurately portrayed evangelism.

So he painted another picture. The scene was similar to the first. It had the same storm—the black clouds, the flashing lightning, the angry waters. There was the same little boat crushed by the breakers, its crew vainly struggling in the waves. In the forefront was the same large rock of safety with the same seaman holding on for salvation. But the artist made one change. Now the survivor was holding on with only one hand, and with the other hand he was reaching down beneath the waves to lift up a sinking friend.

That is the New Testament picture of evangelism—that hand reaching down to the lost with the offer of life. Until that hand is offered, there is no hope—and there is no Gospel. The good news is that God has acted to save a people for Himself.

The Gospel in Person

To know what this means, we have only to look at Jesus. He is the Evangel incarnate—the Gospel alive. For a few brief years He took upon Himself our identity and demonstrated in our midst who God is and how much He cares. Everything He said and did was controlled by His mission. "The Son of Man did not come to be served, but to serve, and to give His life a ransom for many" (Matthew 20:28). Finally He wrapped up all our sins in His own body and bore them to the cross (1 Peter 2:24).

The Gospel concerns Someone, not something. It can never become an abstract theory or mechanical program, since it is an expression of God's love, and God is a Person. Some methodology must be used in getting the message across, but the hand that extends the invitation is flesh and blood.

Perishing humans who come to Jesus and feel His saving grip are no longer their own. We belong to Him who holds us by His grace. And in His ownership, we participate in His mission.

Evangelism thus becomes a natural expression of the church. As the body of Christ (Ephesians 4:16; 5:23, 30; Colossians 1:11; 2:19), we reflect in our individual lives that for which He gave His fleshly body on earth. To live otherwise would be a repudiation of our redeemed nature.

Not to leave the issue in doubt, Jesus told His disciples that as the Father sent Him into the world, so He sends us (John 17:18; 20:21). All who believe in Him now are called to His work (John 14:12). There are no exceptions. Whether we realize it or not, every Christian is a personal demonstration of the Gospel, "known and read by all men" (2 Corinthians 3:2-3).

Enabled by His Spirit

But how can this happen? After all, are we not all mortal beings? How can persons with all the frailties and perversions of corrupted humanity ever demonstrate the life and ministry of Jesus Christ?

The answer to this basic question brings us to the Person of the Holy Spirit. God is the Father in administration; God is the Son in revelation; but God is the Spirit in operation. Wherever God is known, the Spirit is the power by which He works, and Jesus is the Word by which He is disclosed.

Thus the work of making Christ known and loved falls within the sphere of the Spirit's activity. He convicts the world. He calls to repentance. He regenerates and sanctifies the believing heart. He guides into truth. He answers prayer. He helps in infirmities. He empowers for service. In it all, He glorifies the Son, and thereby men and women are drawn to the Father.

Obviously evangelism cannot be legislated by church committees or worked up by highly organized crusades, however well intentioned they may be. Human effort apart from the Holy Spirit is utterly futile. Only to the degree that we allow the Spirit to exalt Christ in and through us can our labors bring forth any fruit.

Our Perfect Example

This being understood, a careful study of the Savior's life will yield the greatest insight to our task. Contrary to our finite experience, there never was any doubt in His mind about the right thing to say or do. People were as open books under His scrutiny (John 2:25; 16:30; 21:17; Matthew 12:25; 22:18; Mark 2:8; Luke 6:8; 11:17; etc.). In His divine nature, He knew all the complications of environmental circumstance and heredity that influence human behavior. And since He also knew perfectly God's will, when He acted, there was no mistake.

Of course, our understanding of His way is always clouded by ignorance. We see only through a glass darkly. But however great our limitations, we can rejoice that we have in Christ a perfect Teacher.

To be sure, our glimpse of Him in the New Testament is very brief. Only portions of about fifty days of His incarnate ministry have been preserved in the gospel accounts. Many things have been left unsaid, and when we finish our study, a thousand questions are still unanswered. Yet that is all the more reason to give earnest heed to those few things that are revealed. Every word is important. Though the inspired picture is sketchy, enough is revealed to see the Master Evangelist at work.

Training Men

Jesus envisioned the day when His Gospel would be heard by "the whole world" (Matthew 24:14). With this in view, He set upon a course that would not fail. The plan progressively unfolds in His ministry, culminating in the Great Commission to His church (Matthew 28:18-20).[1]

His strategy was to prepare a nucleus of laborers for the harvest. These followers in turn would reach others and train them with the same vision. In time, through the process of reproduction, He saw the day when every person would have opportunity to intelligently respond to the Gospel of God's redeeming love.

To show what He meant, Jesus gathered His disciples around Him while He ministered to the world. Hence a few were always learning by observation. Everything that is written in the Gospels is seen through the eyes of these men. We have in these inerrant documents a record of those things that shaped their lives.

Person to Person

There are many scenes of Jesus helping great crowds of people. The common people hear Him gladly. Sometimes those who listen number into the thousands. They are awed by His mighty power and generally respond enthusiastically to His works of deliverance. As long as He satisfies their physical needs, they want Him to be their king.

Yet few of the multitudes become disciples. No more than a few hundred are recognized as followers of Jesus before He returns to heaven.[2] And those who do respond to His invitation seem to come through individual contact. Doubtless the masses were inspired by His public ministry, and it prepared hearts to receive Him, but the real impact of His message came person to person. Mass meetings clearly were not the strength of His evangelism.

The force of this pattern should not be lost by the church today. Jesus is depicted in the Gospels primarily as a personal worker. He deals with people where they are. There is a naturalness about it—no frenzied flurry of activity, no big promotional campaigns, no crash programs to save the world overnight—just the daily routine of going about His Father's business.

Each One Different

Each situation is as different as the people involved. God likes variety. Any attempt to force rigid categories upon human circumstances is dangerous. Jesus does not put people into types.

This should be remembered in interpreting the personal episodes in the Gospels. No two are alike, and we should not suppose that there will ever be an exact parallel in our experience.

However, as we recognize the uniqueness of every personality and circumstance in the Scriptures, we see similar persons and characteristics today. And by taking as our text the whole scope of Jesus' ministry with different people, we can begin to discern certain patterns that will guide our steps in His way.

Plan of the Book

In this book twelve general subjects of personal evangelism are selected for analysis. Each chapter centers on a person or group for in-depth study.

You are asked to first read thoughtfully the Scripture passage. Then read the introductory description of the episode, pausing to consider the probing questions asked as the story unfolds.

If you want to pursue the subject further, move to the next section, which highlights for comparison other experiences of Jesus. These encounters have a similarity or striking contrast with the focused incident that may sharpen your perspective.

Following these inductive assignments, I share some general observations. Feel free to make corrections or add impressions growing out of your own findings.

Each chapter also has a few exercises designed to help

you make personal applications, particularly in regard to methods of face-to-face evangelism. Hopefully, too, you will go on to put into action what you learn.

The book concludes with a general review of principles in Jesus' way of reaching men and women. For those who might wish supplementary reading, a bibliography points you to many additional sources of information.

Read with your Bible in hand. Any translation will do. It would be most convenient if you used a parallel Gospel.

A Practical Concern

An effort is made to direct the study to the most basic questions in evangelism. What is the Gospel? How do you confront people with its claims? How do you lead to a decision? Then what can be done to establish a person in the faith and assure reproduction?

In seeking an answer, note closely the way Jesus did it. At the same time, try to think through the principle in relation to your own witness.

The manual has been forged on the anvil of experience. Each chapter has been developed and tested in evangelism classes and Bible study fellowships over many years of teaching.

Group Experience

While you complete study assignments individually, you can also gain much by sharing your findings within a small group.

That is why you are urged to get with some friends who have the same interest. If desired, the fellowship might be a Sunday school class where the lessons are made an adult elective course.

Leadership can come from within the group, perhaps rotating each week. It is the responsibility of the leader to open the conversation and keep it moving in the right direction. The group leader is like the quarterback in football, leading the team but usually letting someone else run with the ball.

After a period of informal greeting, the meeting may begin in prayer. Then you move into the Bible study, sharing together your observations as time permits. Problems that have arisen through the study can be discussed. The exercise section especially will assist the group in expressing personal feelings. I hope that out of this will come some definite plans for evangelistic outreach.

If someone feels inclined to ask for special prayer, you can unite your faith for the request. Remember that in bearing one another's burdens you fulfill the law of Christ. Also keep in mind the assurances of help from above and do not let a meeting close without giving praise to Him from whom all blessings flow.

Prayer for Guidance

Now as you approach the study, ask God to give you His direction. Open your mind to the instruction of His Spirit. And knowing that the Divine Counselor always lifts up Jesus, fix your gaze upon Him.

Nearly twenty centuries have passed since He walked on the earth in the flesh, but He is still present in the reality of His resurrection. As He reached out His hand to people in the beginning, so He extends the invitation today.

Take His hand. He is the Way. All you have to do is follow.

1

FIRST
DISCIPLES

———•———

Study Focus:
John 1:29-51

Jesus begins His ministry by calling a few men to follow
Him. In turn, these men are with Him as He ministers to
others. Though they were slow to understand, all but one were
destined to become leaders of His church. Read carefully the
account of the first to be selected in John 1:29-51.

The Setting

The time has come for Jesus to make known His mission to the
world. Coming from the temptation experience in the wilderness, He goes to Bethany beyond Jordan where His cousin,
John the Baptist, is preaching. People from all over the country are assembled there to hear the great prophet. The greatest
revival movement in over four hundred years is emerging.

Here Jesus is baptized by John. As He comes up out of

the water, the Spirit of God descends upon Him as a dove, and a voice speaks from heaven, saying, "This is My beloved Son, in whom I am well-pleased" (Matthew 3:17; cf. Mark 1:11; Luke 3:22).

The next day, while passing through the crowd, John identifies Jesus as "the Lamb of God who takes away the sin of the world." It was tantamount to saying that Jesus was the fulfillment of all the promises represented by the blood on Jewish altars for thousands of years. Later the prophet repeats the announcement in the presence of two of his disciples (John 1:35). Imagine how it must have excited the anticipation of the people!

Waiting Disciples

One of them is John, a rather philosophical youth with strong feelings and ambitions; the other is Andrew, older and more pragmatic. Both are from Capernaum where they are fishermen with their brothers. Though different in temperament and ability, each in his own way has a tremendous capacity for helpfulness.

Of course, these men embody their culture. They share its hostility toward Gentiles and Samaritans, while regarding themselves as the chosen people of God. There is little comprehension of the real nature of His kingdom. Yet unlike most of their contemporaries, deep within their hearts is a longing for spiritual reality. Though outside the priesthood and lacking in higher theological education, they are students of Scripture. In particular, they know the messianic promises. That they came to hear the prophet indicates that they are walking in all the light available to them. In fact, probably already they had been baptized by John in token of their repentance. Why do you think that Jesus began His ministry by drawing near to such spiritually alert people?

Approach

As Jesus leaves the meeting, Andrew and John start to follow Him. They must have recognized the significance of The Baptist's introduction, and there is something about Jesus' presence that attracts them. Noticing their interest, the Master turns and kindly asks, "What do you seek?" as if to say, "Is there some way I can help you?"

The two young men hardly know how to reply; yet wanting more information about Jesus, they timidly stammer, "Rabbi, where are you staying?" Not a bad question in light of the circumstances. Wouldn't you like to find out more? If people desire to learn more, they need to know where Jesus can be found.

How He answers them displays in embryo His approach with sincere seekers. "Come, and you will see." What a simple way to answer an inquiry. While pointing out the human obligation to seek the truth, He makes clear that an honest quest will not be unrewarded.

So they go home together. It is the tenth hour (about four o'clock in the afternoon), and the guests probably stay until late in the evening. Think of what it must have meant to share Jesus' hospitality, asking Him questions, listening to Him expound the things of God. As He makes them feel at ease and draws out their own aspirations, any doubts are dispelled about His claim upon their lives.

Can you picture these two men going back to their homes that night under starlit skies, their pulses beating with wonder, their hearts swelling with joy? How would you have felt in their place?

Result

So enraptured is Andrew that he goes at once to tell his brother, "We have found the Messiah." Then to confirm the good news, he brings his kinsman to Jesus. Isn't it wonderful the way new believers spontaneously want to share their faith?

When the Lord sees the big fisherman, He calls him by name and also affirms his worth as a person. "You are Simon the son of John; you shall be called Cephas." Translated, the name means Peter or Rock. It suggests a personality trait that enhances self-esteem, to say nothing of strong leadership. Why would this insight inspire Peter with confidence, both in Christ and in himself?

What they talked about after this is not recorded. As is so often the case in the gospel narrative, we can only conjecture. But we can be assured that Peter did not go away the same.

Emerging Pattern

The next day Jesus finds Philip, a neighbor of Andrew and Peter. Knowing his prepared heart, Jesus immediately comes to the point. "Follow Me," He says. There is no request that

Philip recite a creed or join an organization. All He asks is obedience. Jesus does not ask anyone to believe something they
do not live. Faith is a commitment of life. How does this command reflect the underlying philosophy of our Lord's training
of His disciples?

Like Andrew, Philip cannot keep his excitement a secret.
He tells Nathanael, "We have found Him of whom Moses in
the Law and also the Prophets wrote, Jesus of Nazareth, the
son of Joseph."

Encountering skepticism that anything good could come
out of so lowly a town, Philip simply takes Nathanael to see
the evidence. He takes his friend to Jesus. Again we see how
doubt is overcome by bringing the curious seeker into the
presence of reality.

Observe that both of these men display a knowledge of
the Old Testament Scriptures. Note, too, the tremendous com-
pliment Jesus pays Nathanael by calling him an Israelite in
whom there is no deceit—echoing a pattern of affirming
admirable qualities in people. It also underscores that the first
disciples are spiritually concerned people. What does this suggest about the place to begin a ministry to reach the world?

Doubtless Nathanael, like Simon, is impressed with
Jesus' correct appraisal of his character. When asked how He
knows, Jesus replies that He has seen Nathanael before. We are
not told whether this is a reference to our Lord's omniscience
or some prior discernment, but, however acquired, it would be
appreciated by a stranger.

Nathanael is convinced that he has met "the Son of God,"
but he does not yet understand all the hardships following

Him will entail. Nor does he fully realize that someday his King will be killed. Nevertheless, Jesus assures him that he will "see the heavens opened, and the angels of God ascending and descending upon the Son of Man." Why do you suppose the Master, in the beginning, projected this glorious vision of His coming glory?

— COMPARISONS —

The disciples continue to follow Jesus as He moves out in ministry to Israel. In fact, He lets them help in what He is doing. They take care of His hospitality, providing for His lodging and meals (I haven't found any place in the Gospels where Jesus turns down an invitation to dinner. What a happy discovery! But it was one way some people could exercise their ministry). On their way back from a visit to Jerusalem, the disciples actually become involved in baptizing converts of His preaching.

After a few months, however, they go back to their former occupations. At least, the fishermen are found down by the Sea of Galilee cleaning their nets. There is no evidence of disobedience. They just do not seem to understand the Lord's larger plan for their lives. Read the account in Mark 1:16-20, Matthew 4:18-22, and Luke 5:1-11.[1]

Jesus asks to borrow a boat so that He can go off a little from the shore and address the crowd following Him. When He finishes speaking and the people disperse, He turns His attention to the problem of the disciples. They have fished all night and have caught nothing.

Jesus tells them to go out again and let down their nets in deeper water. Discouraged though they are, they do it on the strength of the Master's word. The new effort results in a fantastic catch, filling to overflowing two boats with fish. Out of this experience, the disciples, and especially Peter, get a deeper insight into themselves and their Lord. What does the incident show about taking an interest in the pressing concerns of people you are seeking to lead?

Jesus seizes the occasion to impress the disciples with their own evangelistic mission. Using the analogy at hand, He calls them to a ministry of fishing for people. "Come, follow Me," He says, "and I will make you to become fishers of men."

Many comparisons between catching fish and catching people come to mind in this figure. What parallels do you see?

These practical lessons in evangelism learned from catching fish are not to be taken lightly. Observe that the applications relate to the call of Christ to follow Him. What is said here simply reemphasizes His initial invitation to the disciples.

In this connection, read the account of the would-be disciples in Matthew 8:19-22 and Luke 9:57-62. Is there any essential difference between His approach with these men and the first disciples? What is Jesus insisting that they do? Why is His demand so urgent and uncompromising?

— OBSERVATIONS —

1.   *Winning disciples who will win others and train them in discipleship is the basic strategy of evangelism. Ultimately this is*

Christ's way of reaching the world. Here then is the priority around which our life must be oriented.

— ο —

2. *The place to begin is where people are open to the Spirit of God. There is no point in trying to kick open a locked door. Go where there is evidence of spiritual renewal and work out from there as the Spirit prepares the way.*

— ο —

3. *Natural relationships among family and close friends often prove advantageous in spreading the Gospel. An inroad into one life may give access to the others.*

— ο —

4. *Public testimony attracts people to Christ. Those who are interested in knowing more can be given the opportunity for further instruction.*

— ο —

5. *Jesus invites the most thorough investigation of truth. The Evangel has nothing to hide. Nor should we. Sincere seekers should be encouraged to look closely at the claims of Christ—and at our lives in Him.*

— ο —

6. *Learning is most natural in a family. Education at its best takes place when teacher and pupil can live together, experiencing practical truth in the context of love and understanding. Such fellowship around Christ provides the atmosphere for follow-up and training of workers.*

— ο —

7. *The personal value and unique gifts of persons need affirmation. Ask questions and offer comments that will help individuals discover their potential. Everyone has some strong points if we will look for them.*

— ο —

8. *We are called to come after Jesus. He demands unconditional obedience to Himself. Whether we understand all the implications of His invitation is not critical. What matters is that we trust Him. By following Him, we will learn in time what He wants us*

to know, including the commission to make disciples. We begin
where we are and move out to the ends of the earth.

— o —

9. *The best is yet to come. Christ had the long view—He saw*
things in the now as they will appear in eternity. When the day
of final triumph comes, the discomforts and trials of our present
labors seem small. We must instill in our followers this vision of
the ultimate victory.

— PERSONAL EXERCISES —

Evangelism begins by following Jesus. The road is different for
each disciple, but the direction is the same. Think back again
upon your journey with Christ, from the time you first met
Him until now.

To illustrate your pilgrimage of faith, take a piece of
paper and draw a line graph depicting your life—your highs
and your lows, times of great exhilaration and times of sorrow—bringing you up to the present. Along the way indicate
by a † where you believe that Christ became to you a real personal Savior. Also draw a fish at the point where you believe
that your witness was used by God to bring another person to
Christ. Be honest. If you are not able to recall an instance of
someone finding the Savior through your life, just draw your
own line as it is—empty.

Turn again to Luke 9:57-62 and reflect on why these good
men hesitated to follow Jesus. Do you see any problems in
your life that hinder your obedience to the call of Christ? If so,
what can you do about it? To put it another way, are there some

practical ways that discipleship for you can become more winsome and contagious?

— GROUP MEETING—

In your group, divide into clusters of four people. Explain your drawing, recounting the time you met Christ and the process that led up to your decision. Then tell about your first experience of leading another person to Jesus, if you have had that opportunity.

When all have had a chance to share, discuss some of the problems that have emerged in your thinking about the excuses men gave to Christ's challenge in Luke 9:57-62. But do not end with the difficulties. Go on to talk about what can be done to enhance the thrill of witnessing. Let everyone have a part.

Close with a prayer of thanksgiving, acknowledging your failures, but praising God for your privileges and the anticipation of "greater things than these."

—ACTION—

With someone else seeking to become a fisher of men, go out and share your faith. If you do not already have such a person with whom you can work, look around in the church for a growing disciple. Likely there is one now waiting for your invitation. Hereafter, try to witness together, and impart to each other your vision and methods in winning people to Christ.

2

RELIGIOUS
GENTRY

———————o———————

Study Focus:
John 2:23–3:21

One of the early encounters of Jesus occurred with Nicodemus. As an example of His dealing with a religious gentleman, this incident is unsurpassed in the Gospels. Read several times the account in John 2:23–3:21.

The Setting

Several months have passed since the call of the first disciples. It is time for the Passover, the feast commemorating Israel's deliverance from bondage in Egypt. All Jews twelve years and older who are able to travel are expected to attend the celebration in Jerusalem.

An integral part of the observance is the offering of blood sacrifices in the temple. Animals for this purpose are sold in the temple area at exorbitant prices. Also each adult male Jew is required to pay annually a half-shekel temple tax. Since only Jewish coins are acceptable, money changers are set up to exchange foreign currency for legal tender. And, as with the blood offerings, the fee for this service is excessive.

When Jesus enters the temple courts and sees how the worship of God is being perverted, He is filled with righteous indignation. Making a scourge of cords, He proceeds to lash the hucksters while loosing the frightened animals and over-turning the tables of the money changers. When the startled Jews demand some "sign" of authority to support His action, Jesus tells them of His future death and resurrection in veiled terms, which leaves them utterly bewildered.

His behavior enrages the Sanhedrin. Jesus is more than a troublemaker; He is set upon a course that threatens to undermine the whole temple tradition. Such reform cannot be tolerated by the corrupt establishment, be they religious or civil officials.

By contrast, the exploited common people are grateful. "Many believed in His name." But typical of the masses, their reaction appears more a yearning for an easier way of life than any change of heart. Jesus refrains from trusting Himself to them.

The Exceptional Person

One man among the elite is deeply moved by the day's events. Nicodemus is a Pharisee, a member of that select group of dedicated Jews who endeavor to keep every detail of the Law. As a teacher in Israel, he is known for his grasp of the Old

Testament Scriptures. His distinction has earned for him a place in the Sanhedrin, the ruling body of the nation. Only seventy men in all Israel hold this honor. Undoubtedly, he is an eminent citizen. Successful. Respected. Devout. What more could a religion ask of a man than Nicodemus has achieved?

Yet he comes to Jesus. Why? To give Jesus some advice? To get information for the Sanhedrin? Or is it because he recognizes something missing in his own life? And why does he come after dark? To escape detection? To walk undisturbed? No other time to come? Or is he so anxious that he cannot wait until morning?

For whatever reason, Nicodemus certainly gives Jesus a high salutation. What does this greeting say about his feeling?

Approach

Jesus brushes aside the nice talk and gets right to the point. He tells Nicodemus that a man must be born again in order to see the kingdom of God. All the outstanding credentials of the proud religious ruler are ignored. Whether or not this Pharisee is awed by Jesus' deeds and words is not important. What matters is his relationship to God.

This is the only time Jesus uses this figure of a "new birth." Why do you think that it would be especially shocking to a pedigreed man like Nicodemus?

Jesus does not talk to him about moral improvement through strict adherence to law and ritual. Rather He speaks of a totally new quality of life infused into one's personality by the Holy Spirit. Just as a person is born into the physical world through natural birth, there must be an equally definite beginning in the spiritual life.

When the response of Nicodemus indicates that he does not understand, Jesus clarifies His previous statement by explaining the difference between the flesh and the spirit. A common analogy with nature is used to illustrate the point. Incidentally, wind is a figure often associated with the Spirit of God, the word coming from the same root in the Hebrew. A man with the training of Nicodemus would have recognized immediately the reference. Still he wonders how a man could be so changed.

Observe the way Jesus gently reminds him of his spiritual ignorance, while still showing respect for his distinguished position. What method does He use?

Jesus then affirms His own testimony: "We speak that which we know, and bear witness of that which we have seen." Why would the appeal to personal certainty command attention from someone brought up in a strong religious tradition?

Clarification

Jesus' witness concludes with a reference to a scriptural incident familiar to every Jew. He compares Moses lifting up a brazen serpent in the wilderness to the way the Son of Man will be lifted up (compare Numbers 21:4-9). The picture flashes back to the time when the children of Israel were visited by deadly serpents as a judgment for their disobedience. There was no natural cure for the serpent's bite. Helpless, the people confessed their sin and prayed for deliverance. In answer to their cry, God told Moses to make an image of the serpent and place it high on a pole in the camp. Those who looked upon this symbol of death would live.

It was truly an extraordinary experience. The whole ceremonial system of approaching God was bypassed. No priest was summoned to hear a confession. No one had to come to the door of the tabernacle with a sacrifice. In fact, a contrite person did not need to raise a hand, even to lift a finger. All that was necessary was to look upon God's offer of mercy. A more dramatic illustration of pure faith in God's Word could not be found in the Bible. Why would the focus of this story get to Nicodemus?

Probably at this point the narrative breaks off in the gospel account, and there follows the commentary of John. In any case, verses 16-18 sum up the condition for knowing the life of Christ. How would you define it?

The alternatives are clear. It is law or grace, knowledge or faith, belief in signs or commitment to a Person—Jesus Christ. Finally we must choose one way or the other. Though Jesus does not press Nicodemus for a decision, inevitably the love of light or love of darkness will prevail.

Response

We are not told if Nicodemus becomes a follower of Christ. What do you think? Perhaps for a while he tries to maintain loyalty both to Jesus and the Sanhedrin. But as the chasm between the two deepens, it becomes increasingly difficult to remain neutral. He is found later still sitting with the rulers when they seek to arrest

Jesus. Reminiscent of the impression made on him during the secret visit, Nicodemus reminds his colleagues, "Our Law does not judge a man, unless it first hears from him and knows what he is doing, does it?" (John 7:51). The remark draws their immediate ridicule, which suggests more courage in standing up for Jesus than appears in his question of procedure.

The last appearance of Nicodemus is after the death of Jesus (John 19:39-40). He and Joseph of Arimathea take the broken form down from the cross, gently wind it in linen cloth with spices, and carry the body to the tomb.

The apostolic company flees in fear from the scene, but Nicodemus is not afraid to reveal his loyalty to Christ. His deed must have invoked the taunting jeers of his former associates. Moreover, by touching the dead body of Jesus, he becomes ceremonially unclean, and thereby he cannot take part in the Passover festivities. The break with the old way of tradition is complete.

Jesus had spoken of a God who so loved the world that He gave His Son to die for us. And like the brazen serpent lifted up, whosoever believes in Him will not perish. As Nicodemus holds the lifeless body of Christ, these words must have come to mind. If he had not embraced them before, surely he experiences them now.

— COMPARISONS —

The rich young ruler is another man of excellent moral reputation who seeks the Master. Read the three accounts in Mark 10:17-31, Matthew 19:16-30, and Luke 18:18-30.

This distinguished citizen comes running to Jesus as He sets out on a journey following His tremendous welcome in Perea. Kneeling before Him, the young man asks, "Good teacher, what shall I do to inherit eternal life?" All his outstanding attainments have not satisfied the deeper yearning of his soul. The ring of true life is missing. How does his question reflect a basic misunderstanding of the place of divine grace in salvation?

Jesus replies by asking why he called Him good and then gives the reason for His question: "No one is good except God alone." Noting the man's knowledge of the Law, Jesus summarizes a few of the commandments that relate to holy character. What effect do you think this has upon the young ruler?

When the man claims that he has always kept the Law, Jesus does not refute his morality. But He reminds him of the one thing lacking in his case—loving God more than his riches. Why do you think our Lord was so direct in pointing out the problem?

The rich youth seems unwilling to face his problem. As he walks away sorrowfully, Jesus uses the occasion to impress His disciples again with the cost of following Him. What is the advantage of drawing a lesson from immediate circumstances?

For a different kind of confrontation with a religious expert, read Mark 12:28-34 and Matthew 22:34-40. Here a Pharisaic lawyer asks Jesus which commandment is foremost. When Jesus responds in words of Scripture, the scribe acknowledges the point. Why?

Recognizing the understanding of the smart lawyer, Jesus tells him that he is not far from the kingdom of God. The man obviously knew what to do, yet nothing is said about any decision. Why do you suppose Jesus leaves the matter here?

—OBSERVATIONS—

1. *Self-righteousness can easily become embedded in moral respectability. Though lacking in any personal transformation of heart, such persons usually adhere to a high ethical code of behavior. They tend to make themselves the center of holiness, not God. Inwardly there is a smug sense of superiority. The real essence of sin and the meaning of grace is misunderstood. For them salvation is thought to be the result of good works or church loyalty.*

—•—

2. *Religious gentry, however steeped in tradition, are still alert to signs of miraculous authority. If for no other reason, they are curious to know what excites people. So much the more when multitudes are moved. One sure way to arouse these church members is to let them see a genuine people's movement supported by the power of the supernatural.*

—•—

3. *Such people are also impressed by the reality of spiritual life. Where it is evidenced, they become curious and hungry. So in talking with them, accentuate the positive blessings of the new birth, such as belonging to the family of God, assurance of sins forgiven, abounding joy and peace now, and the certainty of life everlasting. These are qualities of Christian living that mere conformity to moral law can never give.*

—•—

4. *Personal testimony is intriguing. Religious conformists who have no vital experience with God are dismayed by a vibrant witness of Christ's transforming power. When it comes through in all its beauty and wonder, you have their attention.*

5. *Reference to the Scripture is impressive with those who respect its authority. Religious people usually are nominally committed to the written Word and often have knowledge of Bible truth. It can be used to great advantage.*

—•—

6. *Nothing is accomplished by arguing about one's false standard of righteousness. If it comes up, we are further along by agreeing that the person is good by society's standard.*

—•—

7. *The question is, compared to whom? Christ is the fulfillment of the law, and His life is now our only standard of comparison. That is why all of us are under condemnation. Men and women must be brought to measure themselves by this criterion. Whatever the approach, the principle of evangelism is to get our eyes off ourselves and on to Jesus.*

—•—

8. *When Christ is lifted up, we are made to face the reason for His death. Thus we see the insufficiency of all human efforts to earn divine favor. Redemption by faith in the blood of Jesus Christ comes as our only hope.*

—•—

9. *Obedience to the truth understood is a prerequisite for further illumination. Whatever it is that we know God wants us to do, it must be done. Faith finds expression in active commitment. Herein is the difference between lovers of good and lovers of evil.*

— PERSONAL EXERCISES —

Self-righteous persons, infatuated with their own goodness, tend to compare themselves to less moral people. When witnessing to such a person, what might you say to point out that Christ is our only standard of comparison and that is why all of us are under condemnation?

If you needed to explain the reason for Christ's coming into the world and the nature of redeeming grace, how would you express it? Say it your way, but whatever your preferred method, point to the love of God for a fallen race, that even while we were under the judgment of death, Christ died for our sins and rose in triumph from the grave. Now all who repent and believe in Him shall not perish but have eternal life. It is all of grace—nothing deserved by moral distinction, nothing earned by good works—it is simply a gift of God. If you need help in putting together a plan of salvation, there are any number of excellent gospel tracts that you may consult, such as "The Bridge," "Steps to Peace with God," or "The Four Laws."

To check yourself, write out your testimony. Keep it brief. Simply tell what you were before Christ became real to you, how you met Him, and what has happened since. Make it sharp and interesting. As a suggestion, you might begin with the question, "May I tell you how my life has been changed?" When finished, ask the question: "Have you come to know in a personal way something like this?"

— GROUP MEETING—

In circles of four let each person read his or her testimony. Then honestly react to the way it comes across. Does your witness make clear the need, the provision, and the condition for receiving Christ as a personal Savior? Is the presentation appealing? If not, let the group suggest how it might be stated better.

During this time of sharing, balance criticism with affirmation. Be sure to note in each person's testimony what especially impresses you about his or her faith. Then in closing the meeting, join together in praising God for what He has done.

— ACTION —

Give your testimony to some good citizen of the community who may lack assurance of the new life in Christ. Do not try to pressure the person to make a decision. Just tell what great things the Lord has done for you and watch for an opportunity to say more, should questions arise.

3

SINFUL
WOMEN

———•———

Study Focus:
John 4:1-42

The episode with the Samaritan woman is the longest narrative of personal evangelism in the Gospels. Since the disciples were not present during the initial contact, the conversation was either reported by the woman or by Jesus. However it got to us through the Spirit's direction, the story is unsurpassed for insight into the Master's method. Read it through in John 4:1-42. Then read it a second time, pausing after each verse to meditate upon its meaning.

The Setting

After the Passover, Jesus starts back to Galilee. Due to growing hostility to His ministry among the rulers in Jerusalem, it seemed wise to return to a more favorable atmosphere. Strangely, though, He goes by way of Samaria.

No proper Jew would have any dealings with the Samaritans. They were a mongrel race, produced by union of wayward Israelites with Gentiles following the conquest of the Northern Kingdom by Assyria. Despised by the undefiled sons of Abraham, the Samaritans had developed a corresponding hatred for their neighbors through centuries of antagonism and hostility (compare Luke 9:51-56).

So intense was this enmity between them that Jews traveling between Judea and Galilee tried to avoid any contact with Samaritans. Travelers would cross the Jordan River at the Samaritan boundary and journey along the eastern bank, bypassing Samaria. Jesus at other times followed this route, though for different reasons. But on this occasion He takes the more direct course home.

Coming to the village of Sychar, a town about twenty-five miles from Jerusalem, the weary travelers look about for a place to have lunch. It is noon and they are hungry. While the disciples go into town to buy some food, Jesus sits down to rest on the curb of Jacob's well.

The Woman

A woman comes out from the village to fill her water jar. Strange that she chooses this hour. Drawing water is a chore that women did in the cool of the early morning or late evening. No sensible woman would walk the half-mile from town carrying a heavy water pot during the hottest part of the day. Moreover, at this time she will miss seeing the other women of the village who like to linger at the well to visit while filling their jugs. Is she actually trying to avoid their company?

There is a reason for her to feel shame and rejection in the presence of decent women. She is a prostitute. Her moral looseness is general knowledge around town. Respectable people have no association with her kind.

Doubtless the sight of a man at the well comes as a surprise. Even more, His features and dress differ from those of the Samaritans. He looks like a Jew, perhaps even a rabbi.

Pulling her scarf about her face, she moves quickly to the side of the well opposite Jesus. Fortunately it is wide enough to keep her from rubbing shoulders. Without lifting her eyes, she fumblingly ties the rope to the handle of her container. The jar is lowered into the well, making a splash as it disappears beneath the surface of the water. In a moment she lifts the filled vessel, its cool contents spilling over the well curb.

Approach

"Give Me a drink." In one sentence Jesus' words break the tenseness. Yet what a natural way to open this conversation! He is thirsty, and the woman had water to give. Had He not spoken first, likely the woman would have been too fearful to speak. And by putting Himself in her debt, He is making her feel important—she is genuinely needed. Why do you think that Jesus said nothing to her about being born again?

The woman is dismayed that a Jewish man would ask this favor. Taking the opportunity to explain His mission and using the context of the situation, He tells the woman of living water that He can give her to drink. Certainly Jesus makes what He has to offer sound inviting. How does He do it?

Unable still to grasp the spiritual application of living water, the woman interjects a question that reflects her confusion. It could have led to needless discussion about the origin of the well. But Jesus will not be led astray.

Coming back again to His gift of everlasting water, He contrasts it to the water of this world that cannot permanently quench the thirst. Though one drinks the world's water, he or she will thirst again and again (the tense of the word suggests an endless thirst, reaching even into eternity or hell). But those who drink His water shall never thirst again. His water shall become in them a "well of water springing up to eternal life." How would this positive presentation have impressed you?

Facing the Issues

Whatever Jesus is talking about, the woman wants it. "Sir, give me this water," she says. But as so often is the case, her desire is superficial. She thinks this is a chance to get out of the hard work of toting her heavy water jug.

Shattering her false notions, Jesus asks the woman to go and bring her husband. There is nothing odd about this request, since it was not proper for a woman to receive religious instruction unless it was sanctioned by the head of the house. In this case the request makes her face the tragic failure in her life. Sooner or later one has to come to terms with sin.

Jesus does not go into all the sordid details, but enough is said to prod her guilty conscience. What a gracious way to do it!

Knowing that she is found out, the woman offers her own confession. She is honest, and Jesus does not let it pass without notice. At the same time He indicates that He knows about her situation.

Perceiving that Jesus is a prophet, the woman suddenly reminds Him of the different worship centers among Samaritans and Jews. Her fathers believed that Mount Gerizim was the accepted place, whereas Mount Zion was claimed by the Jews as the hallowed spot. This question had been argued for centuries and was certain to precipitate controversy whenever discussed. Why the woman brought it up is not clear. Perhaps the conversation had gotten a little too personal, and this maneuver was a way of diverting attention from the touchy issue at hand. Or the woman could have been sincerely disturbed by the problem. In any event, Jesus would not be distracted. While acknowledging her point, He interprets it in such a way that she is brought back to the subject of a personal relationship with God. What is the main appeal that touches you from His clarification of true worship?

Convincing as it is, the woman avoids her own responsibility under the pretext that the promised Messiah will come and explain everything. There comes a point when knowledge must give way to faith. So brushing aside all speculation, Jesus confronts the woman with the unequivocal announcement that He is the Christ. It is now a matter of accepting or rejecting the integrity of His word. Why do you suppose that He waited until now to identify Himself?

Response

As Jesus speaks, the disciples, laden with groceries, return from Sychar—without ever getting friendly with the Samaritans. They were amazed that their Master would be speaking with a woman. Apparently it had never occurred to them to share the Gospel while shopping in town.

But the woman cannot contain her secret. She has met the Savior, and in the deep reservoir of His abundant life, she has begun to drink that water that quenches the thirst of the soul forever. Leaving her water pot at the well, she runs back to the city to exclaim her joy. Jesus never did get His drink.

The woman's witness in town provokes tremendous curiosity among the men. Her testimony that Jesus told her everything she had "done" infers that her sinful life is past; she is a new creature. Now there is a new kind of love shining through—a love that draws men, not to herself, but to her Lord. Those who heard her story could not restrain the urge to see Jesus.

Meanwhile, the disciples are trying to get Jesus to eat lunch. It is a perfect opportunity for Him to teach them a lesson about His mission in the world. How does He turn the focus of concern to answer their question?

As He speaks, men are coming from the city walking through the ripening fields of grain. Jesus beckons His disciples to look at the harvest. It is ready to be reaped. He is not referring to the grain that still has several months to mature; the harvest is in the hearts of the men who want to hear for themselves the word of life. No wonder the disciples do not forget this experience. How does Jesus apply it to their own labors?

—COMPARISONS—

Another record of Jesus dealing with a woman overtaken by sin is in John 8:1-11.[1] Read it and try to feel the action.

The incident occurs in the temple courts as Jesus is teaching a group of people gathered about Him. Suddenly some teachers of the law and the Pharisees break through the crowd and throw down at His feet a woman taken in the act of adultery. They want to know what Jesus will say about her punishment. According to the law of Moses, she should be stoned. Yet the Romans had taken away the right of the Jews to inflict the death penalty. The unmerciful accusers see in the situation an opportunity to accuse Jesus of disloyalty, either to the moral code of Israel or to the regulations of the state.

But Jesus will not play their game. Bending over, He writes something in the sand with His finger. Whatever is written, it arrests the interest of the men while diverting attention from the woman. Then Jesus rises and says, "He who is without sin among you, let him be the first to throw a stone at her." And again He stoops down and writes on the ground. What effect do you think this has upon the crowd?

No one is willing publicly to say he is utterly without sin. Condemned by their consciences, one by one the men leave. After all are gone, Jesus turns to the guilty woman and asks where her accusers are. How does His manner call to mind her dignity as a woman and make her feel that she is uncondemned by men?

Surely she is deeply grateful. Calling Jesus "Lord," the woman affirms that she is free. Her Savior concurs. Yet very firmly He reminds her to go and "from now on sin no more." What does this show you about presenting the plan of salvation, especially in getting at the matter of sin?

For another glimpse of Christ's compassion for a distraught woman, read the reference to Mary Magdalene in Luke 8:1-3 (compare Mark 15:40-41). Little is told about her life except that she was delivered from seven demons. However, we know that in gratitude she ministered to Jesus and His disciples.

In this ongoing contact with Christ, note that other women were associated with her. She was not left alone to face the world, nor was she denied a place of service in the church. What principle does this underscore in follow-up?

— OBSERVATIONS —

1. *There are no race or cultural boundaries to the Gospel. Jesus is "the Savior of the world." This being true, we should not let artificial barriers hinder evangelism.*

———•———

2. *There are obvious proprieties that must be respected when dealing with someone of the opposite sex. Jesus showed no embarrassment when speaking with women, but He did not get too familiar. When alone with them, which was the exception, invariably the circumstances allowed no possibility for gossipmongers to get a tale started.*

3.   We should not hesitate to acknowledge our need of help, even if only for a drink of water. Weakness in our physical body is a way of identifying with others.

—·—

4.   A conversation is sure to get attention when we start at the point of the other person's concern. Explanations can then be related to the focus of interest.

—·—

5.   The simplest things of ordinary experience can be turned into spiritual object lessons, making theological truth easier to grasp. The wise soul-winner will try to incorporate commonplace experience in the presentation of the Gospel.

—·—

6.   Listening to people brings their gratitude and affection. It is also a good way to learn what is on their minds. Here is much of the secret of counselingand the sought-after friend.

—·—

7.   Noticing good qualities in people, like honesty or generosity, and commending them for these build respect for our witness. Moreover, if we are discerning, everyone has some noble traits.

—·—

8.   In talking with people, it is well to anticipate responses and plan ahead how to answer. Whatever the person says, we should be prepared with another question or statement that will carry on the theme.

—·—

9.   Marginal issues should be avoided. But when they are injected into a conversation, they can be politely recognized without dwelling on them. As quickly as possible, we should come back to the central subject.

—·—

10. One person excited about Jesus is the best advertisement for the Gospel. Our life can create a mystery that causes others to stand in awe. Even the skeptic is silenced before a living exhibit of God's transforming grace.

—PERSONAL EXERCISES—

Recalling how Jesus appealed to the Samaritan woman, consider some ways that you might speak today with a lonely sinner. For example, you might begin by asking, "Mary, have you ever made the wonderful discovery of Jesus as a personal Savior?"

As a sequence, think of a good way to build upon the preceding statement. Say it your way—words that reflect your personality and comfort level.

Why not write out your ideas? Begin with one that appeals to curiosity, like Jesus did when speaking of the water that always satisfies thirst. Try an appeal that speaks to spiritual need, using the technique of contrast to show the difference between the life Christ gives and that of the world. What might be an appeal to conscience, probing the issue of sin? Can you come up with a commendation of a person while at the same time clarifying the situation? Practice, too, how you can keep a conversation on course by using the technique, "Yes, what you say is true, but . . . " To wrap it up, phrase in your mind an appeal to faith, calling a person to commitment.

—GROUP MEETING—

Divide into groups of four. Discuss among yourselves the various approaches that have come to mind. Let everyone share.

Then pair up and role play a situation. Take turns being the witness. Together you might work out a pattern that draws upon the strengths of each.

Thinking about these appeals has caused you to recall many blessings of God. Let this be an occasion to conclude the meeting by lifting up your hearts in praise to a mighty Savior.

—ACTION—

Befriend someone of the opposite sex who seems overwhelmed with failure. Without improper familiarity, demonstrate your love in a way that reflects clearly the Gospel of Christ. Try to associate the person with another of his or her sex and age who will continue to show concern.

4

HATED
PUBLICANS

———·———

Study Focus:
Luke 19:1-28

M any of the personal dialogues of Jesus recorded in the Gospels are with friendless people. Of these, none is more revealing than the meeting with Zacchaeus. Read the account twice in Luke 19:1-28, with particular attention to the first ten verses.

The Situation

Jesus is on His way with His disciples to keep the last Passover. In a few days He will be taken and crucified. His journey takes Him through Jericho.

This famous city spreads out on the plain west of the Jordan about fifteen miles from Jerusalem. It was a beautiful oasis surrounded by groves of palms and balsams. The export of dates and palm oil made it one of the wealthiest cities of Judea. Here Herod the Great had built his winter residence because of the ideal climate. Since it was located on a main trade route, Jericho was also an important customs station.

Word of Jesus' coming precedes Him, and as usual, a large crowd assembles along the street to see Him pass. Among them is a small man, so short that he had climbed up into a sycamore tree in order to get a good view.

The Person

His name is Zacchaeus. He is the director of the revenue office—"chief tax gatherer." It is his duty to supervise the collecting of taxes imposed by the occupying army of Caesar. Enough money had to be raised, not only to pay the Roman levy, but also to reimburse him for the bribe to get the appointment. Beyond that, everything was clear profit. The Romans did not care how much more was charged, so long as they got their share. Little wonder that publicans became wealthy.

The job, however, cost them the respect of their people. Not only were they resented for their means of acquiring riches, but they were considered traitors to their country, despised for collaborating with the heathen. The Talmud put them in the same class with murderers and thieves. They were deemed unfit to sit in judgment or to give a testimony, and no money received from them could be put in the alms box of the temple.

One can imagine the countless times that Zacchaeus had

felt this disdain. He heard the insults of his countrymen when he walked the streets. Though he had the official protection of Rome and all the comfort that money could buy, he knew that he had no real friends. Kicked out of the synagogue, shunned by his neighbors as "the black sheep" of his family, he must have lived in loneliness and self-pity. How do you think he felt about others?

Approach

When Jesus passes by the sycamore tree, He looks up and notices Zacchaeus. Then, to the dismay of everyone on the street, He speaks to the publican. "Zacchaeus, hurry and come down, for today I must stay at your house."

Can you sense how Zacchaeus felt as he heard these words? Looking down into the face of Jesus, he must have thought to himself, *Jesus knows who I am; He calls me by my name.* What a wonderful thought! Can you recall when that realization first dawned on your soul?

Not only did Jesus convey His understanding of Zacchaeus' situation; He wanted to be with him—in spite of all he knew about the man's unsavory reputation. Jesus was actually inviting Himself home with him. The impression is conveyed that the Son of Man needs to stay in his house. What an overwhelming thought!

Probably no one else had ever shown the tax collector this kind of attention, certainly not the religious people of the city, who were embarrassed even to be around him. But the One the people had come to see is not ashamed for everyone in town to know that Zacchaeus is His friend. Imagine the thrill that must have flooded the tax collector's soul as he thought to himself, *Why, I believe—undeserving as I am, amazing as it is—I believe that Jesus loves me.*

That message breathes hope into the soul of a wayward sinner and gives meaning and excitement to life, the message that we are loved by God, a love that will not let us go. When this truth comes through, the invitation to come to Jesus cannot be ignored. Why?

Nothing is said about all the theological issues involved in salvation. That can be handled later. The request now simply is for Zacchaeus to get down out of the tree and give some hospitality to Jesus. Do you have any idea why in this instance Zacchaeus was not exhorted about his sin?

Response

The publicly condemned revenue agent does not need to think over the proposition. He is convinced that Jesus means what He says. Without hesitation he scrambles down, and right there on the dusty street corner receives his Lord. What a scene that must have been, to see these two men giving and receiving the customary embrace and kiss.

The people are dumbfounded. They cannot conceive of the prophet from Nazareth staying in the house of this notorious sinner. Doubtless some of the uncaring crowd hiss and jeer as Jesus and Zacchaeus walk home together. But what do you think was in the mind of Zacchaeus?

Follow-Up

When they get to the house, a place of more privacy, Jesus has time to talk with Zacchaeus about his new faith. Certainly the man needs instruction. But it is always easier to deal with problems once a commitment to Christ is clear.

One thing they discuss is the matter of restitution for past sins. Apparently there is some question about the ethics involved in the acquisition of the tax collector's wealth. Whatever the shortcoming, Zacchaeus is willing to make it right. Not only will he restore fourfold to those persons he has unjustly charged (in strict accord with the old Jewish standard of restitution—Exodus 22:1; compare Numbers 5:7), but also he determines to give half of his fortune to the poor. How do you see in his resolve the principle of repentance?

Zacchaeus is making a completely new beginning. It would be easy for him to entertain doubts about the reality of his conversion. Observe how Jesus brings encouragement to him and his family by reminding them of their great heritage of faith (verse 9). What principle in counseling new Christians impresses you here?

As He has often done before, Jesus takes time, too, to explain the reason for His mission in the world. "The Son of Man has come to seek and to save that which was lost." How reassuring these words must have been to Zacchaeus. The statement also must have made the disciples ponder what they have witnessed. For this was an object lesson in evangelism— a demonstration of what the ministry of Christ is all about. How would you have understood it if you had been there?

In view of their expectation that the kingdom of God was immediately to appear on earth, Jesus adds a parable to further clarify His mission. He tells of a nobleman giving his servants ten talents to invest while he goes away and then later returning to receive an account. Two of the servants wisely invested the money entrusted to them, but one servant made no effort to return a gain. How does this story reflect upon the investment of Jesus in His followers and their faithfulness in evangelism until He comes again?

—COMPARISONS—

Perhaps Jesus had heard of Zacchaeus from a fellow tax collector, Matthew, also known as Levi. The Master called Matthew during the first year of His ministry in Capernaum. Read the three accounts in Mark 2:13-22, Luke 5:27-39, and Matthew 9:9-11.

Jesus notices Matthew sitting at the place of toll one day as He passes by. Always perceptive of the yearning heart, Jesus says to him, "Follow Me." Nothing more needs to be said. The man gets up, leaves everything behind, and follows his Lord. What similarity do you see here with the response of Zacchaeus?

The joy of personally experiencing the transforming grace of Christ cannot be self-contained. To celebrate the occasion, Matthew invites many of his friends to a feast at his house. Evidently he wants them to meet Jesus and His disciples. How does his desire to share a good thing compare with others who met the Master?

The scribes and Pharisees are indignant when they see Jesus eating with "the tax gatherers and sinners." To eat and drink with people who were careless about the Jewish food regulations was to make Himself unclean. Answering the objections, Jesus explains that showing mercy is more important than mere conformity to rituals. Then telling his critics what this means, He declares, "I have not come to call the righteous, but sinners to repentance." How do you think His words were received by the persons at the feast?

Note that Matthew's account includes Jesus' reference to the Old Testament. Why do you think that detail was so significant to the host of the dinner as well as to the scribes?

The happy way that Jesus and His followers feast causes the long-faced disciples of John the Baptist and the Pharisees to ask why they do not fast. How does Jesus use their question to further clarify His mission?

Later He likens that generation to children sitting in the marketplace and saying, "We played the flute for you, and you did not dance; we sang a dirge, and you did not weep." Look at the picture in Matthew 11:16-19 and Luke 7:29-35. What do you believe Jesus has in mind when He says, "wisdom is vindicated by all her children"?

—OBSERVATIONS—

1. *A zealous soul-winner will always be criticized by some people for mingling with sinners. To the pious legalists such conduct appears scandalous. Yet the outcasts of the religious establishment will appreciate it.*

2.   *We need to be alert to signs of spiritual interest while engaging in the normal pursuit of our vocation. These may appear at any time and amid the most unexpected circumstances, even from the treetops.*

———o———

3.   *There are many ways to single individuals out from the crowd for personal attention, but one of the best is to go home together.*

4.   *People must be made to feel wanted and loved in our presence. When this acceptance is sensed, whatever the means, they will like to be around us.*

———o———

5.   *The invitation to receive Christ is now. Today is the day of salvation. There is no assurance of tomorrow. One needs to respond when the offer comes.*

———o———

6.   *A public appeal for one to step out and identify with Christ can be an encouragement to faith. The act of coming forward, while not necessary for salvation, may express a desire words cannot express. It says to everyone, most of all to the person doing it, that here is someone who means business. However, the gesture must be followed up with personal counsel on the meaning of the act, or response to an open invitation may lead to confusion.*

———o———

7.   *Restitution is a good indication of sincerity in repentance. Unless there is the willingness to make amends where possible, one may question how deep the commitment runs.*

———o———

8.   *Since each person is different, it is important to deal with the particular need. The theological content of the appeal can be presented with this in mind. What is already known does not require elaboration, but that which is unclear calls for explanation.*

9. *Our evangelistic mission needs repeated amplification and interpretation in life situations. After a while those who follow us cannot help but get the point.*

—.—

10. *Someday we must all answer for the way we have handled the Word of life. There will be an accounting when Jesus returns!*

—PERSONAL EXERCISES—

Jesus explained to Zacchaeus and to Matthew that He came to save the lost. This theme recurs in many ways through the Gospels. On one occasion when the scribes and Pharisees murmur about His practice of receiving sinners and eating with them, Jesus told the parables of the lost sheep, the lost coin, and the lost son. Read them in Luke 15:1-32.

Select one of these accounts as an illustration that you might use to show a contemporary outcast how much Jesus cares for the lost. Imagine that you are having dinner together, and the opportunity arises for you to tell this story as if it happened to the person before you. Use the most pictorial language you can, and keep it in modern dress. Conclude your narrative with a question, such as: "Do you see what God's love is like, Jim?"

As an added stimulant, inject midway in the story a question to assure that the person is following your thought, such as: "Do you get the picture, Jim?"

It will be helpful to write out your illustration. Thoughts have a way of untangling themselves at the end of a pen or pencil.

— GROUP MEETING —

Take turns telling your stories, perhaps in groups of four. Discuss among yourselves how each one sounds. If one does not seem sharp and picturesque, make specific suggestions as to how to improve it.

Then join in prayer with the fellowship, expressing your desire to tell in new ways the old, old story of Jesus and His love. And through it all give praise to God.

— ACTION —

Seek out a person despised by others, someone friendless or lonely, and become a friend. Visit at home. Go out together. Invite her or him to some function where your friend will feel wanted. And while you are showing your love, share the story of the infinitely greater love of your Savior.

5

PROUD AND CONTRITE

---o---

Study Focus:
Luke 7:36-50

Contrast makes differences more apparent. This becomes very evident in the persons at the feast in Simon's house. Read the account two times in Luke 7:36-50; first read rapidly to get the feel of the situation; then read slowly, reflecting upon each verse.

The Setting

Jesus is invited to have dinner at the home of a prominent Pharisee. Why a man of his position would ask Jesus to eat with him is not clear. Perhaps he has heard Him preach and is curious to know more about the Stranger from Nazareth. Doubtless, too, he has knowledge of the mighty works Jesus has done in this area. Not long before, the centurion's servant had been healed at Capernaum and the widow's son raised from the dead at Nain (Luke 7:11-17). These miracles, coupled with the witness of John the Baptist (Luke 7:18-35; Matthew 11:2-19), had caused quite a stir in the country. Though the people remained unrepentant (Matthew 11:20-30), Jesus was certainly the main topic of conversation.

The dinner affords an opportunity for members of the town elite to meet the leading news-maker of the day. Still Simon takes care that none of his friends will think he is unduly fond of Jesus. This becomes immediately apparent when the ordinary courtesies extended to a guest are denied Jesus as He arrives. There is no welcome kiss, no washing of His feet, no anointing of His head with oil. Such a slight could not have been missed by the other guests, who probably received the customary greeting. Why do you think that Jesus would put up with such obvious partiality?

Despite the absence of cordiality, Jesus takes His place on a couch beside His host. In typical oriental style, meals were eaten in a reclining position, the upper part of the body leaning toward the table with feet extended outward. Uninvited persons who may have come into the room were standing near doorways. Since the typical banquet hall of that time was partially open to the street and easily accessible, likely a number of men had wandered in to watch.

The Women

Suddenly there is a commotion outside. As everyone turns toward the door, in rushes a woman of the street. She is recognized as a "sinner," a term used to denote a harlot. A gasp of shock spreads through the gathering of respectable citizens. Simon is stunned. The audacity of a degraded woman breaking in upon his party!

Before he can stop her, the woman runs to Jesus and stands weeping at His feet. Tears stream down her cheeks and fall upon His feet. Without saying a word, she bends over and dries His feet with the long tresses of her hair. Then she reaches into her robe and takes out a vial of costly perfume. This is her cherished possession, the means by which she has attracted men to herself. Weeping unashamedly, she breaks the alabaster cruse and pours its precious contents upon the feet of Jesus.[1] While the fragrance of the ointment fills the room, she caresses His feet with kisses.

What is your explanation for her action? Was she already committed to Christ, and was her devotion an expression of gratitude? The lavish display of affection suggests that she had some prior contact with Jesus. Perhaps she had heard Him tell how He would forgive all who came to Him in true repentance and faith. Somehow, though, it is clear that the love of Christ had gripped her heart. The breaking of the little alabaster cruse symbolizes her resolution to break with her sordid past. However expensive the spilled ointment, and in spite of the ridicule society might heap upon her, she wants to show her gratitude to the One who truly cares for her.

Approach

Whatever prompts her coming, Jesus is pleased. He accepts her unashamed worship with tenderness and appreciation.

Though she is castigated by the Pharisees as a "sinner," Jesus does not classify her as such. To Him she is a person who loved much. He feels no need to engage in evangelistic dialogue with her. Why?

The encounter is with Simon, not the woman. While she ministers at the feet of Jesus, the Pharisee is musing to himself that a prophet would have known her condition, and he is incensed that a rebuke is not forthcoming. How does his attitude reflect a twisted concept of the true mission of Christ?

Knowing what Simon is thinking, addressing him by name, Jesus tells a parable of a lender who had two debtors. One owed him ten times as much as the other. When neither had money to pay, he forgave them both. Why would this story be especially appropriate to this situation?

Turning to the host, Jesus asks Simon to tell which of the forgiven debtors would love the benefactor most. The answer is obvious: "The one whom he forgave more." What advantage is there in having the Pharisee say it with his own lips?

Commending him for his good judgment, Jesus proceeds to make the application. Simon could not possibly mistake the forgiven debtor's gratitude with that of the woman. Nor by contrast could he fail to see his own hardness of heart. The Pharisee is indicted by his own words.

Now it is Jesus' turn to pull off the hypocrite's mask. With devastating frankness He calls attention to Simon's moral and spiritual disrespect. How does He do it?

The comparison leaves Simon speechless. He is found out, and in the disclosure of his true self, he is made aware of his perverted values. What is his basic hang-up?

Response

Nothing more is said of Simon. The implication is that he remained as he was—still curious, but unbelieving; quite ready to confess the sin of others, but unwilling to confess his own; unforgiving and unforgiven. Still trusting in his own goodness, he missed the whole significance of Jesus' coming.

But the woman, broken and contrite in spirit, trusting only in the mercies of God, goes away in peace. Literally the word means "go into peace," as if the Savior has opened the gates to a garden of endless satisfaction and rest.

It is an emotional scene, to be sure. Great love is usually filled with emotion. But lest there be some misunderstanding of how salvation came to the woman, Jesus clarifies the reason. What is it?

Surprisingly, the guests at the feast begin to say within themselves, "Who is this man that even forgives sins?" Only God has that power. Clearly Jesus is asserting His divine authority. The line is drawn. Not only Simon, but all the others have to choose whom to believe. Faced with this alternative, from this point on the Pharisees become openly hostile. Why does the gospel differentiation between faith and unbelief in Christ invoke such opposition?

— COMPARISONS —

Luke 10:25-37 tells the story of a certain lawyer who comes to Jesus after the successful evangelistic campaign of the seventy.

He asks the same question as the rich young ruler: How can he inherit eternal life? How does Jesus reply?

By not answering the query immediately, but asking a question of His own, Jesus made the man affirm what he already believed about obtaining God's favor. To the lawyer, of course, it was by keeping the Law.

After listening to the lawyer display his proficiency in his favorite subject, Jesus commends him for his understanding. Then He adds: "Do this, and you will live." How is this student of Scripture now caught in his own words?

Wishing to justify himself, the lawyer asks Jesus to explain who his neighbor is. The reply brings the parable of the Good Samaritan. What a powerful illustration! The contrasting characters seem familiar; nothing is complicated about the plot; the action moves swiftly; it throbs with pathos; the narrative arouses curiosity and holds attention to the end—all marks of effective storytelling.

Jesus concludes by asking the lawyer to express his opinion about the point of the story: "Which of these three do you think proved to be a neighbor?" In replying, the man actually answers the question he initially raised.

Thus, undergirded by the lawyer's own insight, Jesus makes the application: "Go and do the same." Why is further explanation unnecessary?

Another parable Jesus told to certain ones who prided themselves for their righteousness and who viewed others with contempt is recorded in Luke 18:9-14. Here Jesus describes two men who went up into the temple to pray, one a Pharisee and the other a publican. Why does the Pharisee think he is better than others?

On the other hand, the tax collector, standing some distance away, so overcome by his unworthiness that he does not lift his eyes, says, "God be merciful to me, the sinner!" Why was this man justified?

To get more of this method of teaching, note Mark 11:27–12:12, Luke 20:1-19, and Matthew 21:23–22:14. Observe how the Master uses questions to draw out a response, alludes frequently to Scripture, and makes the penetrating applications.

—OBSERVATIONS—

1. *A good place to witness is around a dinner table. It is a natural setting for relaxed fellowship. It is also an ideal occasion to invite friends over for a visit.*

— ◦ —

2. *Tears and kisses speak more eloquently than words. There should be no embarrassment when genuine emotion overflows from the heart. When such expressions of feeling appear, there is usually a deep moving within the soul.*

— ◦ —

3. *Appreciation for acts of kindness inspires greater affection and devotion. Gestures of love must never be ignored.*

— ◦ —

4. *Everyone loves a story. Truth communicated through a parable is more readily perceived and applied. An explanation is always easier to make when it can be illustrated.*

— ◦ —

5. *Questions inviting personal opinion from listeners encourage people to think about what is said. It is a way of stimulating involvement, thus assuring greater application of the message. In the procedure, too, the person addressed can*

voice the point you are making, which is better than for you to state it yourself.

——•——

6.   *Interest in Jesus is not enough. The world has that. There must be a sincere openness to truth and worship of God. Such basic honesty is humbling, but out of it faith is born.*

——•——

7.   *Those who have come to Christ need to hear promises of His forgiveness and peace along with instruction in the power of faith. Particularly is this the case with persons who by their past life of sin find it hard to love themselves. Accenting both the fact and the benefits of grace cannot help but bring joy to a redeemed sinner.*

——•——

8.   *Christian love is convicting. It causes the unloving to feel uncomfortable. One cannot come out unequivocally for Christ without bringing attention to those who remain uncommitted. As long as there is no clear witness, the unbelieving can appear tolerant and friendly.*

——•——

9.   *Gentleness with the weak, severity with the strong— these are marks of a sensitive evangelist. How both traits are blended to present the Gospel tests our understanding of men and women.*

—PERSONAL EXERCISES—

More than fifty parables of Jesus are recorded in the Gospels. Simple enough for a child, yet deep enough for the advanced sage, they present spiritual truth in pictures of human life. Jesus' parables differ from fables, which are generally concerned with ridiculous things. His stories move on a higher plane, dealing with persons and events that can be imagined without transcending reason or nature.

One of the most revealing of these parables was about a farmer who went forth to sow seed. Read the story in Mark 4:1-25, Matthew 13:1-23, and Luke 8:4-18.

Observe the four kinds of soil, each characterizing a condition into which the seed of the Word is sown. Jesus teaches that receptivity to the Gospel varies widely. Like different kinds of soil, people respond to the Gospel differently. There are closed hearts, shallow hearts, distracted hearts, and fertile hearts.

After thinking about these different responses, try to express your thoughts on a piece of paper. Picture the four kinds of soil and illustrate by line drawings what happens to the planted seed.

Making an analogy with your situation today, on the same paper, note under each kind of soil what you can do to assure more lasting fruit.

—GROUP MEETING—

Consider in your group how evangelism relates to the receptivity of the people who hear the Gospel. Let your drawing illustrate what you mean.

As each person in turn shares his or her experience, discuss why an understanding of the soil—knowing the condition of the people you want to reach—is so important in reaping a harvest. Get at the reason the Gospel does not impress all alike.

After discussing these variances in people's receptivity, think about strategies of evangelism that would effectively reach different groups. Obviously the approach must take into consideration their comprehension and willingness to receive the message of Christ. Shape your ideas about the most realistic way to proceed.

Do not dismiss without holding up each other in prayer and exalting the name of your wonderful Savior and God.

—ACTION—

Find someone who needs to hear the Gospel and tell him or her your story. Use language that would appeal to the interest level of that person. If you are asked a question, respond by telling a parable of something contemporary with an obvious application to the issue. If you need to reinforce your story with something even more graphic, try using a pencil to draw an illustration.

6

SICK AND
INFIRM

————o————

Study Focus:
Mark 2:1-12; Matthew 9:1-8; Luke 5:17-26

Often healing of the soul involves healing the body. The paralyzed man brought to Jesus by four friends is one of the most graphic examples. Read thoughtfully the records in Mark 2:1-12, Matthew 9:1-8, and Luke 5:17-26.

The Setting

The mighty power of Jesus has spread across the country. Everywhere people seek Him (Mark 1:37). As the numbers grow, it becomes difficult for Him to move about in the cities. To get away from the press of the crowds, sometimes He goes out into the desert, but still people come to Him from every quarter (Mark 1:45; Luke 5:15-16).

Moving about the country, He teaches in their synagogues, preaches the Gospel of the kingdom, and heals all manner of sickness among the people (Matthew 4:23). A full-orbed ministry to the human need!

When in Galilee, Jesus works out of Capernaum where He stays in the home of Peter. Earlier in this house He had healed Peter's mother-in-law of a severe fever. Needless to say, the fame of His work makes the place a haven for people seeking the Master's touch (Mark 1:29-34; Matthew 8:14-17; Luke 4:38-41).

On this day the house is filled with people, and Jesus is "speaking the Word to them." There is not even room for them all to get in. They block the doorways, overflowing into the street. Even some Pharisees and doctors of the law are there from as far away as Jerusalem. Why do you think the religious experts are present?

While Jesus is talking, there is a startling noise on the roof. Dust and debris start to fall on the hair and beards of the people. As men in the crowd look up, choking for air, they can see sunlight shining through a gaping hole in the ceiling. Suddenly a cot bearing a man is quickly lowered on four ropes and gently laid at the feet of Jesus. If you had been there, what would be going through your mind?

The Person

The man lying on the bed quivers with palsy. Obviously he is an invalid, unable to walk or to take care of himself. Perhaps his disability had been aggravated by some moral failure, which had overwhelmed him with a burden of guilt and remorse. In any case, the inference from Jesus' words is that the man was very despondent.

Still there is in him an element of trust in the Master. At least, he seems to have entered willingly into the plot to get into the house. It might have been his idea in the first place. However conceived, the daring scheme could not work without the cooperation of the four strong men.

This is the beautiful part of the story. The palsied man has four friends who believe with him. In their ingenuity they develop a plan to bring the patient to Jesus. It involves carrying the sick man to the house, ascending to the flat roof by an outside stairway, and tearing open a place through the matted thatch and mud to let down the bed. Of course, the damaged roof will have to repaired. But whatever the cost, they are willing.

Jesus is quick to notice this united demonstration of concern. "Seeing their faith," is the way it is described. What do you think was so impressive? Was it their forethought and planning? Their unity of purpose? Their willingness to get involved—to get their own hands dirty—even to pay for the damages to the roof?

In any event, Jesus says to the paralytic, "Take courage, My son." The greeting shows a tenderness certain to inspire a man lying on a bed trembling in physical and mental fear. Actually the force of the statement is not to urge courage in the face of adversity, as if the man should pull himself together and keep fighting his circumstances. Rather, the words in the original describe an absence of fear altogether.

Then, in the same breath, having quieted the man's emotional anxiety, Jesus tells him why his fear is gone. "Your sins are forgiven." It is an all-embracing declaration. If the condemnation of sin was uppermost in his consciousness, as the words suggest, there is nothing to be afraid of anymore. The root cause of all distress is gone.

Teaching

The theological import of the pronouncement is not lost on the scribes and Pharisees. Immediately they accuse Jesus of blasphemy. Why?

Perceiving their thoughts, Jesus speaks to their evil reasoning. Not that the religious leaders are wrong in their understanding of divine authority, but rather that they are wrong in their rejection of this authority in Christ. Notice how Jesus uses a question to bring out their blindness of heart, confronting them with a dilemma that makes their unbelief even more apparent.

The pious leaders do not answer. Obviously it is easier to restore a body than to heal a soul. But to demonstrate His power to forgive sin, Jesus tells the palsied man to take up his bed and walk.

Apart from supernatural enabling, this would be an impossible request. The issue now turns on what the man believes. Others brought him to Jesus. Now the time has come for him to walk for himself. What principle of faith comes through in this command?

Response

Without hesitation the man obeys. He gets up, throws the little cot over his shoulder, and walks out of the crowded room "glorifying God." His visible physical deliverance confirms that spiritual release that cannot be seen by the eye.

Suppose there had been no outward healing. Would this have nullified the greater miracle of spiritual healing? Again the answer is obvious. Physical health is not essential to forgiveness, and to the unperceiving may even obscure the real need of people. But physical restoration in this case is a temporary means of silencing the opposition to the claims of Christ, though it does not seem to change attitudes of unbelief. Why do you think the scribes remain obstinate?

With the friendly multitudes it is different. They are filled with awe. In their uncomplicated way, the simple people give glory to God and honestly confess that never before have they seen such power given to a man. Why is their reaction so different from that of the religious authorities? If only these authorities could have known more of that deeper power that heals a heart from sin.

— COMPARISONS —

John 5:1-18 records the story of a healing at the pool of Bethesda. The pool was fed by a spring from which the water bubbled up from time to time. Some people thought that this phenomenon was caused by an angel, and in their ignorance believed that whoever stepped into the water first thereafter would be healed.

Hoping to receive this cure, a multitude of wretched people lay around the pool waiting for the imagined stirring of the waters. Of these, probably the worst was a man who had been lame for thirty-eight years. Many times before when the waters stirred, he tried to get into the pool, but handicapped as he was, someone always got there before him. Doubtless he was at the point of utter despair. How does Jesus awaken hope in this man?

The use of the rhetorical question here implies an affirmative response. No one in his right mind wants to be sick. Yet, faced with the blunt logic of his attitude, the man evades the obvious answer and proceeds to blame his illness on circumstances beyond his control. He seems unwilling to take any responsibility for his condition.

Jesus will not let him get by with it. Brushing aside the excuse, He challenges the man to quit complaining and start believing. How does He do it?

The man is made whole, takes up his pallet, and begins to walk. Unfortunately, the healed man's understanding of the Gospel leaves much to be desired. When asked by the Jews why he is carrying a bed on the Sabbath, the man cannot give a clear witness for Christ.

Knowing his problem, Jesus finds him in the temple and clarifies the situation. Note what He tells the man in regard to his past, present, and future. Why do you think the issue of sin was brought up?

For further reflection, read one of the accounts of the man with a withered hand in Mark 3:1-6, Matthew 12:10-14, or Luke 6:6-11. How is his healing similar to that of the paralytic and the lame man at Bethesda?

The same principle of doing something to exercise one's faith comes out in the story of the woman with an issue of blood in Mark 5:25-34, Matthew 9:20-22, and Luke 8:43-48.

However, in this case she touches the garment of Jesus without being told to reach forth her hand. Had He not located her in the crowd and counseled with her personally, she might have thought that there was something magical about His robe. What does He say to her that makes plain the reason for her healing, while also giving an encouraging assurance of peace?

—OBSERVATIONS—

1. *Jesus is concerned for the whole person—body, mind, and soul. Wherever one aches, there He ministers. Following His example, we should not allow the artificial distinction between the physical and the spiritual to have any bearing on our response to a person in need.*

—o—

2. *Most of the physical miracles recorded in the Gospels relate to the healing of the body. Perhaps this is because here human frailty is most evident.*

—o—

3. *Physical healing does not necessarily imply spiritual healing. Yet the Gospel is compatible with good health. The health of the body and mind is impaired when one's conscience is condemned by sin. Undoubtedly this is the reason for much suffering. When the cause is removed, so are the symptoms. However, it should also be clear that ill health does not mean there has been personal moral failure. Many other factors contribute to ill health—including heredity, environmental pollution, accidents, malnutrition, age—to mention only some of the more apparent fleshly conditions.*

—o—

4. *Times of human weakness afford opportunity for learning deeper spiritual truths. Usually people in physical distress*

are more aware of their own limitations, and hence have greater receptivity to divine grace. Jesus utilized these moments of despair to gain spiritual victory. Significantly a large percentage of those dealt with in the Gospels were sick or infirm. A basic rule in evangelism is to be there when people are open to help.

—○—

5.   A positive attitude is especially important when ministering to discouraged people. Jesus does not evade the issue of sin, but He emphasizes forgiveness, wholeness, and peace. His confidence speaks to the emotional as well as to the physical need of the sick.

—○—

6.   Sickness should not be used as a reason for neglecting the claims of Christ. If such is suspected, one good way to get at the problem is to ask a question calling for the person to affirm his or her desire to obey the Lord.

—○—

7.   Faith enters into healing—not a theoretical belief, but a practical expression of trust. We might encourage this action by calling for some realistic response to the Word of God.

—○—

8.   Those who cannot come to Christ need to be brought. Such effort will involve planning and may be costly, but it will bring great reward.

—○—

9.   Persons physically healed must have careful follow-up. The spiritual dimensions of their bodily recovery may not be understood. Only as they are wisely counseled in subsequent fellowship can abiding fruit be assured.

—PERSONAL EXERCISES—

All people sometimes come under physical distress. Whether or not these problems are accompanied by a spiritual need, they hurt. In such a time other burdens may loom larger so that it's easy to become discouraged. Look back upon your own experiences and note what gestures of concern by others have been most appreciated. How does this suggest ways for you to witness when a person is ill?

Put yourself in a situation where you are visiting a sick person. How might you show that you care? As the conversation develops, what could be one way to introduce, without offense, the good news of Jesus?

The use of the rhetorical question has been observed in this lesson, though it is by no means confined to situations of sickness. Using the formula of Jesus as a model, think of several questions that you might use to good advantage in pointing a person to the Gospel. For example, "Mary, would you like to know the forgiveness of your sins?" Remember, whatever you say, the expressed answer is yes.

Having considered this method of securing a favorable response, consider what you would say if the person wants the blessing. What might be a next question you could use to center attention upon the principle of saving faith? For example, "How would you say, Mary, that one becomes a follower of Christ?" (Incidentally, this technique of asking the other person to tell you what is already understood was often used by the Master. As phrased here, it would be a good way to learn what the person thinks while also keeping the subject centered on Jesus.)

Suppose that the person avoids your question and brings up some excuse for not believing. How might you try to confront him or her with the issue? To be specific, what might you do if the person claimed that the difficulties are too great to overcome?

—GROUP MEETING—

Tell what has impressed you most about Jesus' approach in this study. How does evangelism relate to healing of the body? Apart from the miraculous, what did you learn about ministering to the sick?

To personalize it, share an experience when you were hurting and some act of a friend made Christ real to you. Then consider together how you might be more helpful lifting the burdens of others and witnessing to your faith. Bring in some of the ideas coming out of your exercises.

Keep the conversation centered on the authority of Christ, and let your parting be in prayer.

—ACTION—

Visit a sick person and encourage his or her faith. Ask if there is some way you can be of practical help. In the right context, talk about the goodness of the Lord. You might read a comforting passage from the Bible. If the opportunity comes and there is a need, share the way one becomes a Christian. Before you leave, offer prayer for the healing of the body and soul.

7

THE
BLIND

―――――◦―――――

Study Focus:
John 9:1-38

The problem of suffering, especially in relation to physical affliction, is as difficult to answer as it is to ignore. How it relates to evangelism is seen in the experience of the blind man in John 9:1-38. Read this passage carefully.

The Setting

Jesus is in Jerusalem. Again it is the Sabbath. On two previous visits He has aroused the ire of the religious leaders, and this time their anger has reached the boiling point. Jesus has openly declared Himself equal with God (John 8:12-59). The incensed scribes and Pharisees, blinded by their sin, take up stones to kill him.

Yet the time for Jesus to die has not yet come. In perfect calm He walks through the threatening Jews and out of the temple. Outside, among the common people on the street, He is much safer. Why?

"And as He passed by," He saw a beggar beside the road. Such persons swarmed the area, so there is nothing unusual about the sight. What might be considered surprising is that He looks upon the man so intently (the verb in the Greek indicates a deliberate gaze).

The Man

The wretched man has been blind since birth. Never has he seen the light of day. Never has he glimpsed the beauty of a fading sunset. Never has he seen the face of a loving mother. To him the smile of life is hidden in darkness, and there is no hope that the black veil will ever be removed. No one has ever heard of a man born blind being healed.

He must have wondered why this was his fate. The common notion was that physical disability came as a punishment from God for sin. True, ultimately all disruption of God's design in the world can be traced to moral failure. Everyone has sinned. But how could a congenital defect be ascribed to that person's sin, even if personality is pre-existent, as some Jews claimed? Nor does the sin of parents, however real, help a child bear the reproach. Any of the prevalent interpretations only seem to add to his despair.

Dejected, lonely, feeling useless to society, he gropes his way through the uncaring crowd. He cannot see Jesus standing before him, but he can hear the excited chatter of the people. Pleading that someone might have pity upon him, he holds out his hand for alms.

Noticing Jesus' interest in the beggar, the disciples ask Jesus who has sinned in this man's case. They seem more concerned about resolving the theological problem of evil than in ministering to the man's suffering.

Jesus will not be drawn into a lengthy discussion of the problem, although in this case He quickly absolves the man and his parents from blame. Whatever the cause of the misfortune, its removal will show the glory of God. The matter of utmost importance now is to treat the condition without wasting any time. How does Jesus direct attention to the deeper spiritual issue?

Approach

Having affirmed the reason He came into the world, Jesus spits on the ground, makes clay of the spittle, and smears it on the blind man's eyes. Saliva, as well as mud, was considered in that time to have some medicinal effect, so the application may have been understood as a curative treatment. Though unnecessary to a miracle of Christ's healing, it would have encouraged the man's faith. Does this suggest something to you about the testimony of Christian medicine?

It may be well to note that the exercise dirties the hands of Christ. Also, by touching the diseased eyes of the man, Jesus becomes ceremonially unclean according to the strict religious law. But these considerations, so utterly unimportant, properly do not enter into the account.

Jesus tells the blind beggar to go and wash in the pool of Siloam. This place was situated outside the city walls at the southeast corner of town. Why Jesus would ask the man to walk this distance and bathe is not clear. But the journey there certainly must have attracted an interested crowd. In terms of the man's own faith, what purpose does the mission fulfill?

Response

The man follows the instructions. And when he emerges from the water, he can see!

So astonished are the people that some of his neighbors can scarcely believe he is the same person. They take him to the Pharisees, who continue the cross-examination. Then he is brought to his parents, who confirm that he was indeed born blind. Afraid though to tell why he can now see, they suggest that their son is old enough to speak for himself.

So, coming back to the beggar one more time, the Jews try to shake his confidence. But the man sticks to his story. What cannot be denied about his testimony?

The man knows that he can see, but at this point he has only a very limited understanding of the identity of Jesus. All the beggar is sure of is that He must be a prophet. Still, he has no hesitancy in standing up for Him. There is almost a note of humor in the way he chides the Jews, "You do not want to become His disciples, too, do you?"

The inference of his question is more than the Pharisees can take, especially when the healed man points out that only a man from God could open the eyes of a person born blind.

Infuriated, they throw him out. Have you noticed that people often resort to persecution when they cannot deal with facts that undermine their unbeliefs?

Follow-Up

When Jesus hears that the man is excommunicated, He inquires where the man may be found and goes to him. Obviously the restored beggar needs encouragement; he also urgently needs some instruction. Jesus is especially concerned about his belief regarding the promised Savior of God: "Do you believe in the Son of Man?" Clarity here is certainly basic to any future growth in Christ. In the light of this experience, what is a good question for you to ask one who has received help?

Anything the Master says is sure to be accepted by the healed man. After all, Jesus gave him sight. There is no doubt in the man's mind that his Benefactor can be believed. Building in this trust, observe how Jesus brings the eager man to a clear witness of his faith and worship. On this occasion, why would the testimony of Jesus be so effective?

Seeing with the eyes of his flesh and his spirit, the saved beggar becomes now an object lesson to the Pharisees. How does Jesus use his sight to show the blindness of the unbelieving Jews?

— COMPARISONS —

The healing of blind Bartimaeus offers another insight into Jesus' approach. Read the three accounts in Mark 10:46-52, Matthew 20:29-34, and Luke 18:35-43.[1]

This blind man is begging by the Jericho road when he hears a commotion. Learning that Jesus is passing by, he begins to call, "Jesus, Son of David, have mercy on me!" People try to get the man to quiet down, but he persists in his plea.

Hearing the repeated cry, Jesus stops and asks someone to bring the man to Him. At this invitation, the beggar throws off his tattered coat and runs to the sound of Jesus' voice. What does the Lord say to him?

Note that He requests the beggar to name his need. When told that he wants to receive his sight, "moved with compassion," Jesus touches the man's eyes as He grants the request.

The same definiteness comes out also in the way Jesus specifies the reason for the healing: "Your faith has made you well." Why is this important?

A similar story of two blind men is found in Matthew 9:27-31. In this episode, Jesus asks the men, "Do you believe that I am able to do this?" Receiving an affirmative response, He touches their eyes and says: "Be it done to you according to your faith." Word and deed witness to Christ's love.

Observe the same principle in the healing of the worshiping leper in Mark 1:40-45, Matthew 8:2-4, and Luke 5:12-16—as well as the sick woman in Luke 13:10-13. What significance is there in the touch?

The cleansing of the ten lepers recorded in Luke 17:12-19 also might be read. In this instance, however, only one of the ten returned to give thanks to Christ. The other nine went away without knowing the reason for their healing. What a tragedy to receive God's favor in a miraculous act of healing and not understand why!

—OBSERVATIONS—

1.   A powerful presentation of the Gospel is complemented by "signs and wonders." The New Testament breathes this air of the miraculous.

—.—

2.   Invariably miraculous healing attracts public attention to the ministry of Christ. The world of naturalistic law is confounded. Friendly masses generally stand in wonder and reverence; the scornful react in criticism and reproach. But all are made aware that something is happening.

—.—

3.   Not all the sick people of Jesus' day were restored to health, but of those brought to Him, none were turned away. Unfortunately, however, few seem to have become committed disciples.

—.—

4.   Wholeness of the body involves a willingness to have a different pattern of life. Old ways of thinking and acting may need changing.

—.—

5.   Jesus often applies external means in effecting His cure. These gestures might be compared to medical treatment, particularly in a psychological sense. The treatment assures the patient that something is being done to bring a cure. Certainly we should do no less. Rightly understood, there is no conflict between medical science and faith healing.

—.—

6.   God can and often does act supernaturally to restore health. Every person in the will of God has the privilege of appealing to Him for such healing. Where this is done and physical healing does not result, then one can believe that a higher purpose is to be accomplished through the illness.

—.—

7.   Healing of the body points to the greater spiritual healing of the soul. Physical restoration is only a temporary object

lesson of the matter of eternal consequence. To associate deliverance only with the body is to miss the real nature of the kingdom of our Lord.

—◦—

8. *In the spiritual dimension of reality, we must believe in order to see. Hence, those who do not trust Christ cannot possibly understand His claims; they are blind. This is the great tragedy of sin.*

—◦—

9. *Suffering surrounds evangelism with a mystery. Though its presence is not fully explained, the pain may be accepted in the light of Christ's suffering for us. Someday we shall understand that God permits it all for our good and His ultimate praise.*

—◦—

10. *Finally, divine healing consummates in our glorification after death. While it does not yet appear what we shall be, we know that we shall be like Him.*

—PERSONAL EXERCISES—

Picture yourself talking with a woman dying of cancer. Though she has received the best medical treatment available, her body continues to grow weaker. As you talk with her, she asks if her illness has come because of God's displeasure. What would you say?

The question is raised about divine healing. Consider how you might answer, keeping in mind both God's power and His purpose. This is an occasion where your prayer for healing conveys both compassion and faith. Reflect upon the way suffering can be a means of learning what really matters in life.

In the course of the conversation, you learn that the woman

has no assurance of eternal life. Sum up in a simple explanation how she can know that if she were to die, she would go to heaven. Draw upon your whole study in the answer.

Assuming that the woman prays to receive Christ, note several things you can do to help her remain steadfast in the Christian faith.

—GROUP MEETING—

Many basic questions have been considered in the exercises. Let each person share responses to the questions, perhaps reinforcing ideas with personal experiences. Probably some different points of view will surface. In these matters there are no absolute answers, so diversity may help all of you to be more understanding.

Feel free to mention to the group, too, any burden that lays heavy on your heart, even as you listen to theirs. Close by lifting up one another in prayer.

—ACTION—

Remember in prayer someone with a serious physical affliction. Expect a miracle. Yet keep the larger redemptive purpose of God always in view.

As you are able, support your prayer with visible expressions of concern—something you can do to be helpful. However the answer comes, praise God for His grace and wisdom.

8

VICARIOUS
BELIEVERS

———•———

Study Focus:
Matthew 8:5-13; Luke 7:1-10

S eldom does one come to Christ without the aid of others.
Particularly is this evident with persons seriously incapaci-
tated. The centurion's paralyzed servant is an illustration. Read
twice the parallel accounts in Matthew 8:5-13 and Luke 7:1-10.

The Situation

Jesus has just preached the Sermon on the Mount (Matthew
5:1–7:29; Luke 6:17-49). The people who hear the message are
astonished at the way He teaches with authority. And when
He comes down from the mountain, "great multitudes followed Him."

Returning to Capernaum, He is met by a group of Jewish
elders.[1] They have been sent on behalf of a Roman centurion
with the request that Jesus come and save the life of his slave.

The Officer

The centurion probably belonged to the Roman garrison at Capernaum. Some fifty to a hundred soldiers were under his command. As a part of the army of occupation, he represented the imperial power of Caesar.

Usually such men were not fondly regarded by the Jews. But this centurion has endeared himself to the people by generously building for them a synagogue. Very likely he has become interested in their pure worship of God as well as their moral code, which far exceeded anything found in the Roman world. The Jews can honestly say of him: "he loves our nation."

Even more admirable is his compassion, his concern for a slave who is critically ill with palsy. Apparently he has provided the best medical treatment available, but to no avail. When he hears of Jesus, immediately he sends this delegation to ask His help.

The Jews think that Jesus will oblige. As they put it, the centurion is "worthy" of His favor. What betrays their shallow understanding of the way God works?

Approach

Notwithstanding the elders' false view of merit through good works, Jesus says that He will come and heal the slave. They have not gone far before they are met by another delegation, this time "friends" of the centurion. They tell Jesus not to trouble Himself with the long walk because, as the officer said, "I am not fit for You to come under my roof."

Note the contrast in the way the Jews regard the centurion and the way he sees himself. What does this reveal to you about the attitude of the soldier?

The centurion is aware that Jews were not to go into the home of a Gentile. Since he respects their customs, naturally he does not want to embarrass Jesus by asking Him to do something that Jewish leaders might condemn. So he asks only that Jesus say the word, and his servant will be healed. After all, why bother in coming when a command would accomplish the same purpose? As one accustomed to receiving and giving orders, the centurion knows that a word of authority must be obeyed.

When Jesus hears this statement, He marvels and tells those following Him that He has not yet found such faith in Israel. What is faith to the centurion? And considering the situation, why would the human example of a Roman officer arrest attention of the Jews?

Teaching

Authority and obedience belong together. The centurion is under the orders of his superior. His time is not his own. His style of life is dictated by his office. Everything he says and does conforms ultimately to the decree of Caesar. In subjection to this rule he has command. The authority he has over others is possible because he is himself obedient to authority.

On a different level, the centurion recognizes that this is also true of Jesus. He is simply doing what God wants. Because of His relationship with the Father, what He says must be obeyed. Belief in the power of His word is the only logical response to His authority. The centurion knows that Jesus is Lord and simply acts accordingly.

Using his faith as an object lesson to the crowd, the Master Teacher explains how people from all nationalities will sit down with Abraham, Isaac, and Jacob in the kingdom of heaven (note Psalm 107:3 and Isaiah 49:12). By contrast some of the Jews would be cast out. Why would these allusions to Scripture be particularly appropriate in this situation?

Response

Turning to the centurion's friends, Jesus tells them to go their way. The officer believes, so what he asks will be done. Why do you think that Jesus does not come with them as they requested?

"And the servant was healed that very hour." The physical distance between Jesus and the palsied slave is no barrier to the power of God, as the friends of the centurion soon discover. When they return to the house, the sick man is whole.

In a deeper sense, the Roman officer also experiences a miracle. Though he asks nothing for himself, in seeking the healing of his servant he finds the Lord of his own life. What does this suggest about the blessing that comes to those who intercede for others?

—COMPARISONS—

Only on two occasions in the Gospels is it said that Jesus marveled: once at the Gentile centurion's faith (Matthew 8:10; Mark

6:6), and once in reference to the unbelief of His hometown neighbors at Nazareth (Mark 6:6). What do you make of this?

Read the story of the nobleman and his son in John 4:46-54. In this scene the father goes to Jesus with the request that He come and heal his boy who is at the point of death. Apparently the royal officer, like many others, based his faith on what he could see. How does Jesus point this out to him?

However weak his reason, the nobleman senses that Jesus is the last hope for his son, and in his desperation cries out, "Sir, come down before my child dies."

Perhaps something happens in his heart as he says these words. In any event, Jesus tells the father to go, for his son lives. How is this assurance like that given to the delegation from the centurion?

The man obeys and goes his way. It is not a sign that makes him go; rather it is now faith in Christ's word. Learning later that his son is healed, as Jesus said, the nobleman and his whole household believe.

Mark 7:24-30 and Matthew 15:21-28 tell the story of a Canaanite woman's entreaty for her demon-afflicted daughter. On the surface Jesus' response to the woman's plea for help is perplexing. Three times He seems to reject her, first by silence, then by asserting that His ministry is only to the lost sheep of Israel, and finally by the seemingly harsh remark that it is unfair to give to dogs bread intended for the children.

Some imagine that His rebuke is only a playful way of acknowledging the woman's foreign nationality. Some see in it a test of her faith. Some believe Jesus did not want to get involved in a ministry beyond Israel. Still others think that He might have been playing a part in order to expose the prejudice of His disciples. Perhaps if we could have seen the twinkle in His eye, as did the woman, an interpretation would not be so difficult. How do you see it?

Apart from your explanation of His approach, the fact remains that her persistent request is finally granted. Her mother's love would not be denied. What impresses you about her faith?

While thinking of believing for persons unable to believe for themselves, consider the restoration to life of Jairus's daughter in Mark 5:21-43, Matthew 9:18-26, and Luke 8:40-56. In this instance, the father came to Jesus, fell at His feet, and implored Him to come to his house where the little girl lay dying. He believed that the touch of Jesus' hands would restore his daughter to health. But before Jesus could get to the home, some people met Him with the news that the girl was already dead. How did Jesus react to this apparently hopeless situation?

When He arrived and found a crowd of mourners "loudly weeping and wailing," He put them out before going into the room of the child. Then with Peter, James, and John, along with the mother and father, He went into the inner chamber, took the girl's hand, and told her to arise. Why do you think He left the others outside?

—OBSERVATIONS—

1. *Faith in the Person of Christ is the fundamental prerequisite for prevailing prayer. To doubt His Word is to question the reality of communion in His Spirit.*

2. *Faith inspires faith. One person believing creates a posi-tive climate that will influence others. Unbelief also tends to be contagious. Where there is massive doubt, as in Nazareth, miraculous works of God are rare.*

———

3. *The believing person must pray like Christ, which is to pray in His name. Any resistance to His desire must be resolved; all sin must be confessed. This implies both a knowl-edge of His will and obedience to it. As we are in accord, noth-ing is impossible in prayer.*

———

4. *Intercession for others is our greatest ministry in evan-gelism. Especially is this evident when there is no other way to help those who cannot help themselves. We have a partic-ular responsibility for dependent children and servants.*

———

5. *God can only be approached in the knowledge of our unworthiness. No one too proud to take off his shoes can stand in His presence. It is a humbling experience. The sense of our helplessness is intensified by the magnitude of the request.*

———

6. *Love constrains such prayer. Since it is seen only by the Father (not paraded before men), the way we intercede is probably the greatest index of devotion in our work.*

———

7. *An intercessor identifies with the persons lifted up to Christ. In a vicarious sense, we "feel" with them, bearing their sorrows and carrying their griefs. Such a burden will not be easy to bear. There is a cross in it—the willingness to take their suffering as our own.*

———

8. *Usually it involves some practical steps in communicat-ing love. At least, every effort should be made to provide the best aid available in the way of human resources, whatever it takes. Here we are on the spot. What we do will not go unno-ticed by God.*

9. *How prayer can influence another person is not explained. All we are told to do is pray and believe God. Certainly He who holds the world in His hands can do as He pleases. Even what appears to us as inviolable human freedom is at His command. It remains a mystery, but we can see that prayer does change things.* —.—

10. *If we but knew, all of us are the product of others' faith. Generations of prayers have preceded us. In the ultimate sense, we are the fruit of Christ's own intercession. He believed for us when we could not believe for ourselves.*

—PERSONAL EXERCISES—

Before faith can be expressed on behalf of another, someone must care about that person. Think back over the accounts of such concern that you have studied. List on a piece of paper the traits you believe should characterize true friendship.

When you have written these desired qualities, think back upon your life and note persons who have demonstrated those virtues. Recall some specific examples of their love for you.

Relating the qualities of these people to intercessory prayer, how do you see these traits expressed in your burden for others? More personally, define what vicarious faith means—that is, believing for another.

Recall some promises of Jesus that pertain to prayer requests for persons in need. For example, Matthew 7:7-11; John 14:13-14; 15:7; 16:23-24. Try to recite from memory some promises of Scripture that are especially meaningful to you. If you cannot call to mind some verses, resolve to memorize two this week and meditate upon them in your prayers.

It has been said that evangelism has to do more with pleading *for* souls than in pleading *with* them. What do you think is meant by this, and how does it apply to you? Are you meeting the conditions for effectual prayer?

—GROUP MEETING—

Discuss your insights into the nature of genuine love and vicarious faith. You might talk about some of the people who have faithfully prayed for you. This would be a good place, too, to cite some promises of prayer that you have memorized.

With this background, relate your experiences of prayer in bringing persons to Christ. Admit your failures. Affirm your blessings. Share your burdens.

Then go around the group with each person suggesting how together you can help lift the load. Close by joining hands and hearts in intercession for these needs.

—ACTION—

Believe God for someone who does not believe. Remembering, too, that intercession reflects a practical witness of love, find a way to express your concern.

However difficult the situation, do not let disappointing circumstances nor passing time discourage your faith. With God nothing is impossible. So keep looking to Jesus with anticipation and thanksgiving.

9

LITTLE
CHILDREN

———————o———————

Study Focus:
Mark 10:13-16; Matthew 19:13-15; Luke 18:15-17

Children cannot be overlooked in evangelism. Jesus' tenderness in dealing with them and their parents is a lesson as necessary for us to understand as the way He called His first disciples. A good place to see His method is in Mark 10:13-16, Matthew 19:13-15, and Luke 18:15-17. Prayerfully read the three accounts.

The Setting

The story probably takes place in Perea, near the end of our Lord's active ministry. Multitudes of people continue to seek His healing and listen to His teaching (Matthew 19:1-2; Mark 10:1). His high esteem among the common people is seen in this incident that shows Jesus interacting with some of the parents in the crowd.

Deeply moved by the work of Jesus, they bring to Him their babies that He might lay His hands upon them and pray for them. Imposition of hands was a ceremony used often in parental blessings. It conveyed a familiarity and love along with a bestowal of authority.

As noted previously, other persons had brought sick children to Jesus. But the little ones in this account do not appear to have any physical malady. They are presented by the parents solely because of the spiritual benefit believed to come through such a service.

Very likely these people have only a meager understanding of Christ and His kingdom. Still they reverence Jesus as a prophet, and they want the favor of God upon their children. How would you compare their attitude with that of the masses of religious people today?

The Disciples

The surprising revelation in this encounter is the way the disciples react. They seem bothered by the interruption, and they rebuke the parents. Apparently they do not realize the honor implied by the request. Nor do they seem to have any appreciation for a children's ministry. In their view, Jesus has too many other more important things to do. How is your attitude different from theirs?

When Jesus sees the behavior of His disciples, He is indignant. How can they be so insensitive? The ensuing drama demonstrates a truth they will never forget.

Approach

Jesus calls the children to Him. While they are coming, He voices His deep fondness for them. "Permit the children to come to Me, and stop hindering them, for the kingdom of God belongs to such as these. Truly I say to you, whoever does not receive the kingdom of God like a child shall not enter it at all."

Can you imagine how this statement gives the children a sense of acceptance and worth? Without going into any theological explanation, Jesus says that the children characterize His reign of authority in the kingdom. Think of the feeling of importance that gripped them! They are somebody special. How they must have loved this attention!

Jesus does not leave His message to words. Reaching out His big hands, He takes the children in His arms and blesses them. What they may have missed in His prayer, they can understand by His touch, His hug, His caressing of their hair. Why do you think loving physical contact is so much a part of His method with children?

Teaching

The little ones receive Christ's blessing, but the force of His teaching settles upon the older persons present. He reminds them of a disposition in children that all must emulate. In fact, He says that no one can get to heaven without it.

What this attitude is, we are not told in so many words. But in looking at the manner of a child, we have an illustration. What do you think Jesus had in mind? Was it a child's playful humility? Teachableness? Uncomplicated trust? A boundless exuberance of spirit? Their adoring love? How would you sum it up?

Theological truth usually falters when put into definitions. The reality is always greater than the word description. Perhaps that is why we are left to ponder the full import of this embodied example.

Response

No attempt is made to invoke in these infants a commitment. They are too young to understand its meaning. Yet in their innocence, they can know the love of Jesus and rest assured in His blessing. After praying for them, Jesus departs the country.

The parents are left with the responsibility of nurturing their children's faith. Doubtless the experience through which they have come will help them in their continuing task. But they cannot leave the little ones without direction. Each boy and girl will need to confirm individually a childlike faith in Christ upon becoming an adult. Why is the shepherding care of children by parents and other counselors critical in child evangelism?

—COMPARISONS—

On another occasion a child is used by Jesus as an object lesson of saving faith to His disciples. Read the narrative in Mark 9:33-37, 42-50, Matthew 18:1-14, and Luke 9:46-48.

In this instance the disciples are disputing among themselves as to who is the greatest in the kingdom of heaven.

Noticing the argument, Jesus asks them a question that gets the matter out in the open.

When He hears their concern, Jesus reminds His disciples that any person who would be first must become a servant of all. Then to illustrate His admonition, He calls a little child to Him, takes the lad in His arms, and says, "Unless you are converted and become like children, you shall not enter the kingdom of heaven." What does He mean by this?

He has laid down a principle: Conversion of an adult to childlikeness is a condition for salvation. Enlarging upon this concept, Jesus specifically mentions humility in characterizing greatness in His kingdom. Why do you think this trait was singled out above others?

In some way these little ones represent what haughty men and women in their struggle for position trample underfoot. As such, children stand in marked contrast to the selfish ambition of this world. In spite of their lack of prestige and power, children and those of whom they are an emblem are to be received with the graciousness becoming our Lord. As He said, "Whoever receives one such child in My name receives Me." What an astounding analogy!

With this relationship in view, a fearful punishment awaits "whoever causes one of these little ones who believe" on Christ to stumble. "It is better for him that a heavy millstone be hung around his neck, and that he be drowned in the depth of the sea." Anything that would hinder their faith must be put away, even if it requires plucking out an eye or cutting off a hand. We can hardly imagine more graphic language. Despising little children is like despising God, for in heaven their angels always behold His face. Apply this to child nurture.

The Father in heaven wants none of His little ones to perish. To this end, Jesus has come to save the lost. Like the man who has a hundred sheep and discovers that one has gone astray, he leaves the ninety-nine to go in search of the one that is straying. How would this parable impress His disciples?

As already noted, most of the gospel instances of vicarious faith for healing relate to fathers and mothers and their children. Not only does this underscore a special parental responsibility, but it also points out a special privilege. In this connection, how do you interpret the family promise in Acts 16:31?

—OBSERVATIONS—

1.   *There is a quality of life about little children that illustrates the kingdom of heaven. They may not be aware of the Gospel, but in their dependence upon others for care, they reflect a basic attitude of those who renounce self-sufficiency and depend upon the grace of God for salvation. Similarly, in their teachableness and tender conscience, they possess a disposition characteristic of the Spirit-led pilgrim. Perhaps most significant is their love and trust of their parents and other members of the family—a trait that, in its higher spiritual reality, typifies every person within the bonds of Christ.*

—•—

2.   *A child is under the protective care of God. With one in this state of innocence, it is not a question of being outside the*

kingdom of grace, but rather of choosing the kingdom when the decision must be made as an adult.

—.—

3. Children become adults when the purpose of life is understood. This may be called the age of accountability. For some it may come much earlier than for others. It is the theoretical point in a child's development when the issue of God's claim upon one's life can be intelligently confronted.

—.—

4. At this time a child must make a responsible commitment to God. With those who have been nurtured in the faith, it may simply bring into focus what has been assumed all along. With others it may come as a radical redirection of life. However the choice may be expressed, all that is good constrains the emerging adult to freely yield his or her newfound independence to the sovereign will of God. The decision is hard for a proud person—to become childlike in faith—but there is no other way to live in God's family. This willful turning to the Lord may be called conversion—which is the climax of a process beginning with the first promptings of the Gospel.

—.—

5. It is important that children learn the Gospel early while their hearts are sensitive to the divine Spirit. They need to make their choice to follow Christ before a pattern of independence has been hardened by age.

—.—

6. Children need a shepherd to lead them. They are led, not driven, to Christ. It is unwise to try to induce decision through highly charged emotional appeals and pressure tactics. The problem in reaching children is not in getting response but in bringing them to see clearly what commitment to Christ means.

—.—

7. Little children interpret the Gospel mostly in terms of what they experience. Obviously the love and correction they have at home is the most formative influence. Parents are the

key. Any evangelistic effort that has to bypass them is put under a great disadvantage.

———•———

8. *All children of God start as newborn babes in Christ. They need parental care to grow up in their faith. Because children are immature does not mean that they are irresponsible. It does, however, underscore the necessity of continuing follow-up.*

———•———

9. *Children may lead adults to Christ, particularly parents. Sometimes they are the only way to get through to the adults. Nothing is quite so disarming and irresistible as a child's uninhibited love.*

— PERSONAL EXERCISES —

The influence of the home in the development of values cannot be overly stressed. Here we have impressions of Christ and the church that are not easily forgotten. As you reflect upon your childhood, think of the person who influenced you the most in becoming a Christian, even if you were not converted until later in life. Why does this person stand out?

Still thinking of this outstanding person, in what practical ways did he or she help you to feel the love of Christ? Scratch your brain. For example, do you remember the person talking about Jesus or praying with you or showing tough love in the form of discipline?

If you grew up in a Christian home, was there some time during the day when the family observed worship together? What ingredients of that experience do you recall with appreciation? If you have not known a family altar, what would you like to see practiced?

Unfortunately, many persons today have grown up in a dysfunctional family, possibly aggravated by divorce, alcohol, drugs, or a debilitating illness. Often there has been physical or mental abuse. You may have had such an experience and recall aspects of your childhood with sorrow. As you look back, what do you most regret? How much of the problem was your own fault?

Of more immediate concern, you may be going through a less than ideal family situation right now at home, perhaps raising a child as a single parent or coping with an uncaring spouse. If this is the case, try to show your children how Jesus ministered to you, even when you were unloving to Him.

The imperative of helping children develop self-worth in God's sight has been noted. How do you see yourself cultivating this attitude in others?

—GROUP MEETING—

Discuss your ideas about a wholesome Christian home. Perhaps you are facing some troubling family problem. If so, why not share it with the group? This would be a good time to unburden concerns for loved ones and friends.

But move beyond what is wrong to the solutions. Consider ways you can make your home a better reflection of what the church is to be.

When finished, join in praise to God for your relationship in the household of faith. Before leaving, embrace one another with big hugs, and as you do, mention some outstanding qualities in their lives that have been a blessing to you.

—ACTION—

Notice the children around you and make them feel your love. Laugh and play together. And while with them, tell a story about Jesus.

If not acquainted with their parents, by all means seek them out and introduce yourself. This could be the open door for a growing friendship and witness.

10

DEMONIACS

———°———

Study Focus:
Mark 5:1-20

Conflict with demonic powers in this world is no mere academic matter in evangelism. These evil spirits may at times possess human beings and control their activity. Jesus frequently confronted such people. Read one of the most vivid of these experiences in Mark 5:1-20. Parallel accounts may be found in Matthew 8:28-34 and Luke 8:26-36.

The Setting

Jesus has received wide acclaim during His Galilean ministry (Mark 4:1, 36; Matthew 8:18; Luke 8:4). So great is the clamor of the multitudes that He seeks some privacy by going to the other side of the lake.

On the way across, a fierce storm suddenly arises. The frightened disciples entreat Jesus to save them from perishing.

When He commands the wind and the sea to be at peace, His followers are filled with wonder at the way even the elements of nature obey Him.

Arriving at the eastern side of the lake, the party comes ashore under the steep cliffs near Gadara. It is part of the region called the Decapolis because of the ten cities there colonized by Greek-speaking outsiders. Fear of contamination with these pagan elements kept most Jews away.

The Men

No sooner do they disembark than two naked men rush toward them.[1] These two have roamed the area like wild animals, eating what they could scavenge from the swine that grazed nearby and sleeping in the cave-tombs among the bones of the dead. Their pitiful shrieks can be heard day and night. No one has the strength to tame them.

They are demoniacs, meaning that their personalities are under the mastery of an evil power. In this case, many demons have entered them. We do not know how they became afflicted. It would seem that either willfully or in weakness they have been seduced by unclean spirits, and they continue to obey them so that now they have lost control of their own wills.

The effect of their demonization is the destruction of human character. They are brought to complete isolation from friends and family, stripped of their moral integrity, and reduced to a state of utter physical degradation. These men are a terrifying picture of what can happen when satanic forces have their way.

Approach

Though they are driven by devils, despised by society, loathsome even to themselves, still Jesus loves them. He is not afraid to come to their desolate habitation. Where such compassion is present, it is the demons who fear.

The demoniacs cry out, "What do we have to do with You, Son of God? Have you come here to torment us before the time?" The sound is that of a man, but it is the thought of a demon. When evil spirits encounter Christ, invariably a reaction seems to occur. Why?

Other persons have tried to restrain the deranged men by binding them with chains. Perhaps this explains why they asked to be spared further torment. But Jesus does not seek merely to restrain the evil; He gets to the real problem. Speaking directly to the demons, He tells them to come out. There is authority in His voice. Just as previously He had commanded the disturbed forces of nature to be calm, now He shows His power to still the storm in the ravaged mind of human beings.

Jesus asks the spokesman, "What is your name?" Whether He was addressing the man or the demon is not clear, but in any case, it is a way of establishing the identity of the person.

One man replies, "My name is Legion; for we are many." Perhaps this is a nickname by which he is commonly known. Though not very flattering, the name is descriptive of his condition. Yet the use of the singular "my" and the plural "we" in the same breath reflects something of his inner turmoil.

A Lesson

The demons know they must go. However, they ask Jesus to let them enter into the herd of pigs feeding on the mountain. Rather than being assigned to the abyss, they prefer to dwell in some living organism. Why this is desired is not explained, but Jesus agrees to the request.

Immediately the two thousand infested swine panic. Squealing hysterically, they stampede over the cliff and drown in the waters below. The astonished men who are tending the hogs flee into the city yelling the startling news.

Much speculation has arisen as to why the destruction of these hogs would be permitted. Doubtless the spectacle had a strong psychological effect on the released demoniacs. Here was tangible evidence that their tormentors were destroyed. As to the material loss incurred by the pig raisers, it may be well to note that this business was illegal in Hebrew territory, irrespective of the foreign settlers who largely populated the country. The most memorable explanation of this incident is one I recall from an old teacher who said with a smile that he supposed this was the first time devils had ever tried to ride hogs, and they didn't know how to steer them.

Response

Whatever the explanation, when the citizens of Gadara hear what has happened, they come out to see Jesus. They observe the former demoniacs sitting at the feet of their Lord, clothed and in their right minds.

The people become frightened. Further clarification of the details by the eyewitnesses only make them more afraid. They have something on their hands with which they cannot cope. Outcasts of society are being made whole. And the hog owners' illicit investment is being destroyed. What is the tragedy of their reaction?

Obsessed by their earthbound perspective, they ask Jesus to depart from their coast. One can only wonder if some of them also were under the influence of demons, at least some kind of evil deception.

Jesus does not stay long in a place where He is unwelcome. Acceding to the people's request, He gathers His disciples and walks down to the boat.

The healed demoniacs want to go along, too. After all, for years they have been discriminated against in their community. But Jesus tells them, "Go home to your people and report to them what great things the Lord has done for you." Why do you think He sent them back?

The men go away as Christ asks them—back to those who have rejected them before, back to the familiar paths to tell the good news to those who knew them best. It will be hard, but Jesus assures them that people are waiting to hear. So by faith they go.

As they tell their story, people everywhere marvel. The limited training of the witnesses is no serious handicap. What they lack in polish is more than made up by the joyful ring in their voices and the sparkle in their eyes. They can show people the scars on their wrists and ankles made by the shackles of their past bondage. Look! They are free!

Interestingly, when Jesus comes back to visit the same region a few months later, multitudes of people want to see Him (Mark 7:31-37; Matthew 15:29-31). Whereas before they begged Jesus to leave, now they plead for Him to stay and minister to their needs. And as other suffering people are healed, they go out and declare, "He has done all things well" (Mark 7:37). What made the difference?

—COMPARISONS—

Another dramatic release from demon control is recorded in Mark 9:14-29, Matthew 17:14-21, and Luke 9:37-42. In this account a father brings his demon-afflicted son for healing, but the Lord is away on the Mount of Transfiguration. The disciples who are left behind try to cast out the alien spirit, but with no success.

At this point Jesus returns, and the people run to Him. Seeing their excitement, He asks what is going on. The dejected father comes forward, kneels before Him, and tells his story. What similarities do you see in the condition of his son and that of the Gadarenes?

Having heard the pitiful narrative, Jesus, seizing the moment to underscore a deep concern, says, "O unbelieving generation, how long shall I be with you? How long shall I put up with you? Bring him to Me!"

When He sees the boy, the evil spirit throws the helpless victim into a convulsion, and the boy falls to the ground, rolling about and foaming at the mouth. Jesus asks how long this has been happening to him. Then He again listens patiently while the grief-stricken father tells more of the details of his son's affliction, concluding with a plea for help. How does the Master respond to his request?

The father replies that he believes, but needs help in overcoming unbelief. On the surface, his statement seems to be a contradiction. What do you think he means?

Jesus seems pleased at the father's honesty. Turning to the boy, He addresses the unclean spirit directly, "I command you, come out of him and do not enter him again."

The defeated spirit obeys, though not without a final struggle, which leaves the child utterly exhausted. Tenderly Jesus takes the lad by the hand and lifts him to his feet.

Later when Jesus is alone with His disciples, they ask why they could not cast out the demon. It is an opportune time to teach them again a much-needed truth. What is the lesson?

—OBSERVATIONS—

1. *In this world are demonic beings and influences with which we are in mortal conflict. As incorporeal spiritual beings, they are called in the Gospels such names as "demons," "unclean spirits," or "evil spirits." Satan, the archenemy of God, is their leader. In their network of super-human intelligence and communication, they form a kingdom of evil in opposition to all that is holy. To ignore their strength and to be unmindful of their ways would be contrary to the ministry and teaching of Christ.*

—•—

2. *Demonic force is always negative. In their essence, demons are anti-Christ. They seek to implant destructive thoughts and engender rebellion. These evil powers cannot*

create, but unless restrained, they can tear down and corrupt what God has made good.

———•———

3.   Not surprisingly, some mental and physical anguish can be attributed to demon affliction. The gospel writers carefully distinguish between demon-caused diseases and those that are not (for example, Matthew 4:23-24; 8:16-17; Mark 1:34; Luke 4:40-41).

———•———

4.   A demon can enter and leave the body of a person. One evil spirit may bring in others, spirits even more wicked, so that the individual's condition may become worse. Sometimes they gain such control that the victim loses his or her own personality.

———•———

5.   How a person becomes demonized is not disclosed, but it would seem the result of weakness in the face of demonic attack. Most references to this problem in the Gospels refer to adults, but the fact that innocent children also are sometimes involved indicates that demon affliction can occur in childhood.

———•———

6.   Demons know that they are defeated by Christ, whom they recognize as the Son of God, the Lord of heaven and earth. In this respect, they have more sense than those who question His deity. However, demons may not want to admit their subjection. Asking a demoniac what he thinks of Jesus may give some indication of the problem.

———•———

7.   Where demons are in evidence, they can be addressed. One approach is to ask for their names. They may direct a response into the consciousness of the victim or speak directly. The confession of some specific sin may disclose an identity.

———•———

8.   Christians have authority to cast out demons. Evil spirits can be commanded to leave in the all-powerful name of Jesus. Sometimes it may be necessary to bind many together

and assign them all to the pit. Challenging them may precipitate a struggle, but where faith refuses to yield, demons must obey the Word of God.

—•—

9. Persons freed from this bondage need special understanding and encouragement. They should be counseled to fix their attention on Christ, their mighty Savior, and witness to His wonderful grace. Demon attacks may still come, and if one is not vigilant, reinfestation can happen (Matthew 12:43-45). The best safeguard is to keep the void filled with the Holy Spirit day by day in a walk of obedience.

—•—

10. Needless to say, exorcism is full of danger—not just in recognizing the problem, but in becoming preoccupied with it. Awareness of the enemy must not dampen the joy and excitement of following Christ, in whom we are more than conquerors.

—PERSONAL EXERCISES—

The encounter between demonic power and the authority of Christ has received considerable attention in recent years, particularly in reference to evangelism. Not everyone has the same perspective, of course. One of the most difficult aspects of the subject comes out in the area of discernment—knowing how to recognize satanic power when it is present. More especially, how might it appear in a highly affluent society that has a church heritage? Try to sum up your thoughts in a sentence. Before answering, reflect on John 8:43-44; 12:40, 2 Corinthians 4:3-4, and 1 John 4:1-3.

At several significant periods in the training of the disciples, Jesus gave them power to cast out demons. Put yourself in their place, and affirm the authority you have as stated in the ordaining of the twelve disciples in Mark 3:14-15; the sending of the twelve in Mark 6:7, Matthew 10:1, and Luke 9:1; the report of the seventy that demons were subject to them in Luke 10:1, 17; and, finally, in the command to go and preach the Gospel to every creature in Mark 16:15-17.

It would be refreshing to recall some of the assurances of Christ's victory over Satan and the demonic world. Meditate upon such passages as Colossians 2:15, Ephesians 1:22, 1 John 3:8; 4:4, and Revelation 12:10-11.

— GROUP MEETING —

Discuss together your answers to these questions. Let everyone express an opinion freely. Especially share any personal experiences with this problem.

But do not dwell on the demonic. Rather rejoice in your victorious position in Christ. To reinforce your testimony, cite from memory a promise from the Word.

On this note of assurance conclude with a season of praise in the mighty name of Jesus.

— ACTION —

Remembering someone who is hostile toward Christ, pray that God will open the person's eyes to the light of the Gospel. Plead the blood of Calvary. When the opportunity comes for a personal witness, radiantly affirm your faith and experience in the living Savior.

11

CONDEMNED CRIMINALS

———————o———————

Study Focus:
Matthew 27:33-50; Mark 15:25-37; Luke 23:32-47

The ultimate choice every person must make comes to a climactic focus at the cross. Read slowly the account of the crucifixion in Matthew 27:33-50, Mark 15:25-37, and Luke 23:32-47, pondering especially the confrontation of Jesus with the two malefactors in Luke 23:39-43.

The Situation

The hour of the Lord's last suffering has come. Bearing in His blameless body the sins of the race, He is driven to the place of execution at Golgotha. Two other condemned men walk with Him, also bearing crosses.

A large crowd follows the procession outside Jerusalem's gate. Probably some came just to see the spectacle. It is to them great sport—watching the slow, excruciating torture of human life. The rulers of the Jews and the scribes also are there to hurl their vehemence and mockery upon these disturbers of the peace. Insensitive to it all are the Roman guards dispatched to carry out the execution. When not engaged in their duty, they amuse themselves by throwing dice at the feet of their bleeding victims. The mourners present, mostly women, stand by, helplessly weeping.

They all look on as Jesus, like a lamb led to the slaughter, willingly lays himself upon the wooden cross-beams. They listen to the heavy sound of the hammer pounding spikes into His hands and feet. They see the upright cross hoisted by the soldiers and finally dropped with a thud into the hole. Yet He opens His mouth only to pray, "Father, forgive them; for they do not know what they are doing."

Nailed to each man's cross is a paper describing the crime for which he is dying. We are not told what is written on the other two, but inscribed on the center cross is the charge: "This is Jesus the King of the Jews."

As He hangs there, writhing in pain, the chief priests say in derision, "If You are the Son of God, come down from the cross." That Jesus would not save Himself from this terrible death seems the height of folly. Even the malefactors crucified beside Him join in the reproach. What do they fail to understand?

Two Men

Possibly, until today, the two criminals have never seen Jesus. Their impression of Him is formed largely by His manner now.

We might think they would show more sympathy, seeing they are under the same sentence. However, in their case death is a just penalty for their deeds.

One of the outlaws, railing in his bitterness, asked Jesus, "Are You not the Christ?" He has heard this said in the mockery of the people. So he raises the question himself and then orders, "Save Yourself and us!"

If what they say is true, the felon demands that Jesus do what is expected by the world. He does not affirm any faith in Jesus nor show any remorse for his sin. His only thought is for his own physical deliverance. Even for this he casts complete responsibility upon God. After all, he reasons, if Jesus is so powerful and loving, let Him stop all this agony. In what way is this attitude reflected in the world today?

There is no reply to this arrogant disposition. The Savior does not add to the unrepentant man's suffering by further condemnation. He has not come to condemn the world but to save it. How do you account for His silence? Does this suggest to you a way to deal with your antagonists?

A Different Approach

But after a while something begins to happen in the heart of the other criminal. Sensing the tragedy of what is taking place, he takes the side of Jesus and defends Him against the taunts of his fellow outlaw. In the process he affirms his fear of God's justice while confessing his own sin: "Do you not even fear God, since you are under the same sentence of condemnation? . . . We are receiving what we deserve for our deeds; but this man has done nothing wrong." What do you think causes this change in his attitude?

With a broken and contrite spirit, the believing thief says, "Jesus, remember me when You come in Your Kingdom." Somehow in their suffering together, without saying a word to the man, Jesus had imparted the feeling of a first-name relationship.

The dying thief does not request deliverance from the sentence of death, which he recognizes is just. Nor does he have any idea that his Lord will escape death, innocent of sin though He is. He knows that they will all die. There is honest realism here. But what lifts the spirit of the dying man is belief that Jesus has a kingdom beyond the grave. Unexplained, veiled as it may be, he knows that there is going to be a resurrection. And in that spiritual anticipation, he asks to be remembered by the King in His coming glory. In true repentance and faith, the dying thief contritely places his soul in the care of Jesus.

Teaching

Jesus' reply is one of beautiful assurance: "Truly I say to you, today you shall be with Me in Paradise." What a comforting promise! They will go into the future together. There is no speculation. No uncertainty. No delay in salvation. That very day His dying friend will be with Him in Paradise.

The Jews commonly used the term "Paradise" to describe the place of the just after death. It would be easily understood by the thief as a description of blessing to come.

What makes it most appealing is the personal fellowship—the redeemed will be "with" Jesus. That's what heaven is like. Why is such a positive word so appropriate in this situation?

Follow-Up

Nothing else is said by the thief to his new Friend hanging beside him. But he listens to Jesus lovingly commend His mother into the care of John. As the day wears on and the darkness sweeps over the earth, he hears the cry from the cross, "My God, My God, why have You forsaken Me?" Later he hears the same suffering voice say, "I am thirsty." When the soldiers thrust up a sponge full of vinegar to the Savior's mouth, he hears the victory shout, "It is finished!" followed by the committal of His spirit into the hands of His Father. Imagine how these words from the cross reinforced the faith of the new child of God.

The feverish eyes of the thief turn to see Jesus drop His head; then his Savior's eyes close. The blood-drained human body hangs limp upon the blood-red cross. That crimson stain speaks more eloquently than any words—He has given all He has for those he loves. No one saw it more clearly than the dying malefactor.

Soon he, too, dies as the soldiers come and break his legs. But when that shattering moment passes, he enters into a new world. There waiting to receive him is his King. He does not have to pass over Jordan alone.

—COMPARISONS—

In striking contrast to the two outlaws, Pilate is at the top of the social ladder. He is the ruling Procurator of Judea. He is married to Caesar Augustus's granddaughter, and in Rome he is associated with the aristocrats of society. His present assignment is a far cry from what he was accustomed to at Rome. Still it could be a stepping-stone to a more prestigious position. Thus it is important to him that nothing happen to upset the province. He would have preferred to avoid the episode with Jesus. But when he cannot, he tries to disclaim responsibility for the way things turn out.

Read the accounts of his cowardly stance in John 18:28–19:16 and Matthew 27:11-26 (other records in Mark 15:1-15 and Luke 23:1-25). When questioned about His kingdom, what does Jesus point out about the relationship of truth to faith in His Word?

Though Pilate knows that Jesus is innocent of any crime, note how he refuses to stand up against the wrath of the Jews. Does popular support make rejection right? Can the public gesture of washing his hands of the whole affair erase Pilate's guilt? Whatever his denial of blame, it is his consent that sends Jesus to the cross.

What shall we say of the priests and elders who plot Christ's death? Can they be excused because they do not actually sign the decree?

And what about the multitudes that cry, "Let Him be crucified!" Is their loveless scorn absolved by the prompting of their leaders? Do they not all choose Barabbas? How does their decision reflect the attitude of the world toward Christ today?

The change of this attitude in one of the men crucified beside Jesus has already been seen. But there is another person there who has something of a conversion. The centurion who commands the Roman soldiers acknowledges Christ as the Son of God. Quite a reversal of attitude. By the way he permitted his prisoner to be shamefully treated during and after the trial, we know that initially he is callous toward the whole thing (John 19:1-5; Mark 15:16-19; Matthew 27:27-30). What happens at Calvary to change his mind? Read Mark 15:39, Luke 23:47, and Matthew 27:51-54.

—OBSERVATIONS—

1.   *The cross brings into bold relief the purpose of our Lord's ministry. When He took upon Himself our flesh, He assumed our liability and judgment. At Calvary we see its consequence and are made to face the awful fact of our sin. Yet equally clear is the revelation of God's grace—He loved us even while we were sinners.*

—.—

2.   *Ultimately every person must come to the cross and answer the question: Who is this Man hanging between two thieves? And why is He there? Some response must be made. To ignore the crucified Savior is to reject Him. No one can be neutral at Calvary.*

—.—

3.   *Jesus does not try to defend Himself before embittered men and women. Nor should we. A stinging answer to the mocking questions and disdainful curses of unbelievers is silence.*

4.   *Enduring mental ridicule and physical torture without vindictiveness gives to the world a witness stronger than words. Though people may pretend not to notice, their consciences will not let them forget.*

—◦—

5.   *Persons who suffer together may develop a close relationship. Trouble presents an opportunity for evangelism possible in no other way.*

—◦—

6.   *While there is life, there is hope. However deep in sin one may have gone, God will not despise the prayer of a believing heart. The dying thief proves that a deathbed conversion is possible, though we have only this one instance of it in the Gospels—and possibly this was his first time to meet Jesus.*

—◦—

7.   *Turning from sin in repentance and trusting Christ is the sole condition for salvation. Nothing more was required of the believing malefactor. Baptism, the sacrament, good works, a discipline of prayer and Bible study, church attendance—all these things are needed in Christian obedience, but they are not the point of entrance into the kingdom.*

—◦—

8.   *A dying man longs to hear the promises of heaven. How comforting is the assurance of Christ's presence when a loving disciple walks through the valley of the shadow of death.*

—◦—

9.   *To the very end of life, evangelism should be a passion. As Jesus shows us, there is no discharge in this calling, not even in the closing moments of death.*

—PERSONAL EXERCISE—

Reflect upon the question Pilate asked the people, "What shall I do with Jesus who is called Christ?" It was a good question, though Pilate was unwilling to face the issue himself. If you were asked that question today, how would you reply?

Think back upon the two thieves crucified beside Jesus, and reflect upon how all of us, like them, sooner or later must respond to what happened at Calvary. With this in mind, draw a cross on a piece of paper, which will make a dividing line down the middle. Write on one side of the upright line reactions of the unrepentant thief and on the other side the contrasting reactions of the thief who believed on Christ. You should come up with half a dozen or more differences in their attitudes. If you prefer, you can sketch your impressions with line drawings or symbolic figures.

Realizing that the masses usually follow the path of least resistance, how can you help people face up to their moral responsibility before the cross? Be realistic. In this light, locate the problem Jesus faced with the multitude in Matthew 9:36-37. Now describe the solution in Matthew 9:38. Relate this to your ministry.

— GROUP MEETING —

Discuss the two ways that everyone must someday respond to Jesus. Use your drawing of the cross to illustrate your thoughts.

With this background, discuss Jesus' experience with the multitudes. Are you facing much the same situation today in evangelism? Talk about it in your group. More importantly, decide what you can do about it.

Out of this will come concerns for more workers with the mind of Christ, which can be the subject of special prayer.

— ACTION —

Go to a prison or home for the indigent and talk with some lonely soul about the heavenly kingdom. Do not criticize or condemn any that might be unsympathetic. Just open your heart and pour out the love of Jesus. Before leaving, gather up the burdens of each person and lift them to the Lord. And do not hesitate to return again upon their invitation.

12

CHIEF
OF SINNERS

———o———

Study Focus:
Acts 9:1-31; 22:1-21; 26:1-18

Paul said that he was "foremost of all" sinners saved by Jesus (1 Timothy 1:15). Yet after his conversion, no man became a greater blessing to the church. Read thoughtfully the record of his confrontation with Christ in Acts 9:1-31, 22:1-21, and 26:1-18.

The Situation

The incident takes place about four years after Jesus' death. Since the resurrection of Christ, His ascension, and the outpouring of the Holy Spirit at Pentecost, Christian witnesses have been boldly proclaiming the Gospel throughout the land. Beatings and imprisonments have only made them more zealous.

Already the Jerusalem believers are five thousand strong, including a number of the priests. One of the Christian leaders is Stephen, a man full of wisdom and the Holy Spirit. So penetrating is his preaching that the Jews cast him out of the city and stone him to death. As he dies, much like his Savior, this first martyr of the church cries out, "Lord, do not hold this sin against them!" (Acts 7:60). Standing by, holding the cloaks of those who hurled the rocks, is Saul of Tarsus, the chief prosecutor for the established religion.

Under the leadership of this devout Jewish zealot, the church is harassed day and night. His cohorts hunt down followers of Christ wherever they can find them, breaking into their homes and dragging men and women away to prison. To escape the persecution, many of the believers fled to distant regions of the country, and everywhere they "went about preaching the word" (Acts 8:4).

A report comes to the high priest that some of the disciples have taken refuge in Damascus. Saul is dispatched with letters to the synagogue leaders authorizing him to bind any of the Way and bring them back to Jerusalem for trial. With a small detachment of soldiers, he sets out determined to arrest the Jesus heretics.

The Man

Walking along the road, he is easily recognized as an officer of the Sanhedrin. He gained the position through his scrupulous attention to religious duty. A strict Pharisee, he is blameless according to the righteousness of the law.

No Jew of his day is better prepared for world leadership. Born of Hebrew parents in Tarsus, a free city, he has the

advantage of Roman citizenship. His early experience in the
area of Antioch also makes him conversant in the culture of the
Greek-speaking world. He had been sent to Jerusalem to the
school of Gamaliel where he received the finest theological
education that could be given a young man in his tradition.

The implications of the cross are painfully clear to him.
By its judgment all people are declared to be sinners without
regard to the works of the law. Redemption is simply an act
of God's forgiving grace. In receiving Christ, Jew and Gentile
are made one. He is convinced that if this new sect is not exter-
minated, Christianity, unlike other deviant groups in the
Jewish community, has the potential of revolutionizing their
society.

How Saul acquired his knowledge of the Christian faith
is not known. It does not seem that he had any personal
acquaintance with Jesus before His resurrection. Apparently
his information came through contact with Christians and listening to their proclamation of the Gospel. What impact do
you think Stephen's witness at his death had upon Saul?

Approach

Suddenly the men on the Damascus road are arrested by "a
light from heaven, brighter than the sun, shining all around"
them (Acts 26:13).[1] The astonished company fall to the ground
in fear. How might the way Jesus gets their attention compare
with a display of God's power today?

As the stricken men lie trembling on the ground, Jesus
speaks to Saul in his Hebrew dialect. Calling him by name, He

asks a question that makes the persecutor face his misguided conduct: "Saul, Saul, why are you persecuting Me?"

Saul's conscience is goaded with the awful knowledge of his misdeeds. He is known by this awesome Presence that speaks. Recognizing the superiority of the Speaker, he calls Him "Lord," though he does not know Him. "Who are You?" he asks.

Clarification

The voice identifies Himself: "I am Jesus the Nazarene, whom you are persecuting." Why do you think Jesus uses His human name and refers to the actual place where He grew up when answering? Why be so literal in witnessing?

Saul is shattered with the realization that the Person whose ministry he has vehemently sought to destroy—the One condemned by the Jews, crucified as a criminal, buried in a tomb—is indeed alive as His disciples claim. In this moment of revelation, Saul's elaborate anti-Christian structure collapses into ruins. He sees in an instant his perverted understanding of truth. How can he ever correct the wrong he has done? Fully aware that he is accountable, yet willing to place himself under the command of his new Lord, he asks what he should do. How does Saul's response indicate complete faith in Christ?

Jesus tells him: "Arise, go on into Damascus, and it shall be told you what you must do." Doubtless there are many things Paul would like to know, but for the moment obedience simply means continuing on his journey. Why do you think Saul is given this instruction?

Response

Saul does not need to be coerced. Though blinded by the dazzling light, he immediately gets up, takes the hand of someone, and walks into the city. Coming to the house of Judas on Straight Street, he waits in prayer, without sight, neither eating nor drinking.

Meanwhile, God speaks in a vision to Ananias, a disciple living in Damascus. The devout man is told to go to Saul and deliver a message. A bit apprehensive, he is assured that the former opponent of the church is a changed man. Isn't it wonderful how God prepares people to give converts encouragement and direction?

The obedient disciple does as he is told. Entering the house, he tenderly lays his hands on the new believer and says, "Brother Saul, the Lord Jesus who appeared to you on the road by which you were coming, has sent me so that you may regain your sight, and be filled with the Holy Spirit." What stands out to you in this greeting?

Ananias then tells Saul that he has been appointed to know God's will and to experience by sight and sound the presence of His Lord. "For you will be a witness for Him to all men of what you have seen and heard."

Encouraged by these words, after baptism, immediately he began to proclaim Jesus. But soon the persecutor becomes the persecuted, and he has to flee for his life. How is he protected and nurtured during the harassment of his early Christian life? Read 9:23-31.

— COMPARISONS —

Paul, the apostle, was told that he would bear the name of Christ before the Gentiles and the great and small of Israel. To the end of his life, this is what he did. Read again the closing account of his testimony before King Agrippa in Acts 26:19-32. How would you describe "the heavenly vision" to which he remained obedient?

Note how Paul insists upon both the known witness of historic fact and the testimony of Scripture. Observe, too, how he reminds the king of what he knows to be true. What does this suggest to you about presenting the Gospel?

Agrippa is almost persuaded to become a Christian. But like so many others, he will not obey God. So near, yet still he is lost. Never again does he get so close to the kingdom.

By contrast, Paul, standing in chains before him, is altogether convinced. What is more, he dares to wish for every person a commitment equal to his own. Can you say that?

Shortly before his death, Paul writes Timothy a pastoral letter in which he again shares his testimony. Read 1 Timothy 1:12-17 and sum up what impresses you most about this witness.

In his last letter, Paul charges Timothy to be faithful to the truth learned while they were together. Meditate upon 2 Timothy 3:14-4:8. Why do you think he stresses personal association, both his own and that of his family, along with the Scripture, in knowing what to do?

He goes on to remind his young disciple of the judgment when Christ returns. Against this background he mentions some priorities to remember in his ministry. What are they?

Paul concludes with a farewell testimony (verses 6-8). Again he speaks of the judgment to come at the return of Christ. But there is no fear. Rather he looks to that day with great anticipation, not only for himself, but for all who love the coming of the King. Why?

—OBSERVATIONS—

1. *Some have claimed that Paul on the Damascus road had a sunstroke or epileptic seizure, which resulted in a hallucination. The theory, of course, fails to explain the complete change in his life. But if these critics were right, we should earnestly pray that more people have such afflictions.*

—◦—

2. *Sinners must become aware of the awesome reality of God's presence. The Christian witness should create something of this mystery. Until this is sensed, the scoffer is not likely to listen to what we say.*

—◦—

3. *Every person has a sinful past that can be recalled under the convicting power of the Holy Spirit. Hope lies in facing the truth and seeing the utter futility of resisting Christ, the Son of God.*

—◦—

4. *Jesus lays claim to the totality of our lives. He is sovereign over all. To receive Him as Savior commits us to follow Him as Lord.*

—◦—

5. *After Paul affirms Christ as Lord, the question of knowing His specific direction still remains. Here follow-up is*

essential. By continuing in prayer and the Word, listening to the counsel of Christian friends, considering particular circumstances, and unflinching obedience to the Spirit of God, we can know what God wants us to do.

—.—

6.   *New Christians, whatever their associations, must be welcomed as brothers in the family of the church. This loving fellowship provides strength and comfort for every child of God.*

—.—

7.   *The redeemed are chosen vessels and are under His appointment. He has a perfect plan for each one. Within the particular calling of His purpose, all are witnesses of those things seen and heard in Christ. Someday each of us must give account for our faithfulness.*

—.—

8.   *As sinners saved by grace, like Paul, we can never get over the wonder of it all. The remembrance of who we were while in sin, against the knowledge of what we now are in Christ, causes us to praise His name forever.*

—PERSONAL EXERCISES—

A concise summary of Paul's strategy of reaching the world by multiplication is 2 Timothy 2:2. Memorize it.

Observe how the sequence moves from Paul to Timothy to faithful men to others. Four reproducing spiritual generations.

You start, of course, with a Timothy—someone providentially drawn into your life by God. Usually such persons already have some natural association with you, like a family member, neighbor, close friend, or fellow worker. Not that you are the only one involved in their discipleship, but that you have a significant role. Who are your Timothys?

Now look at how they are reaching persons in their sphere of influence. As you have shared with them, are they passing on the vision to a few faithful men or women? This is where your investment begins to pay off.

The real impact of your life, however, becomes apparent when the persons touched by your Timothys start reaching out to others. That's when you can be assured of making reproducing disciples.

How does this pattern unfold in your life? Reflect upon the way persons in whom you have given largely of yourself are now imparting your vision to their disciples and teaching them in turn to do the same.

Recalling Paul's farewell message to Timothy, what would you say to one of your disciples if you knew this would be your last message. Try to put your thoughts on paper in the form of a letter. You need not show the composition to the person, but keep it as a reminder of your present aspirations. Then sometime in the future, take it out and read again what you consider to be your highest priorities today.

—GROUP MEETING—

Come to grips with a personal strategy of evangelism that will assure continual outreach. In view of Christ's mandate to make disciples of all nations, what is a realistic plan to follow? Compare Paul's strategy with that of Jesus. Though they operate in a different context, observe the similarity of the principles underlying both ministries.

Discuss the implications of this approach in your own situation. Be honest with each other. Consider what effect this plan would have if practiced in your church.

After everyone has expressed a view, turn to your farewell letter. Go around the circle and let each person read the message he or she has written. Then join in affirming your commitment to Christ and His calling in your closing prayer.

—ACTION—

As you have seen the need for more workers in the harvest, select another person to go with you to witness. Likewise, the one who has been with you thus far can do the same.

Continue to seek opportunities to share the amazing news of God's redeeming grace. Never look back. The best is yet to be!

REVIEW

M ost of the more detailed gospel accounts of Jesus' personal evangelism have been treated in the course of this study. From these and the gospel narratives as a whole, some general principles emerge in the way He ministered. As you read the summary, check the conclusions against your own. If you agree, check the box before each statement. Probably out of your review will come some refinement of the principles. What really matters, though, is that your understanding find expression in practice.

1. JESUS BECAME A SERVANT TO PEOPLE.

Here His incarnation intersects our lives; it is the foundation undergirding all His ministry. In Christ, God's love is clothed with flesh. Until we become vulnerable to human heartbreak, compassion lacks substance.

☐ *He goes where people can find Him.*

He travels the crowded roads. He visits the big cities and small villages. He teaches in the marketplaces and on street corners. He attends public services in the synagogues and the temple. Though there are times when He seeks to get away from the crowds, usually He is accessible to people looking for help.

☐ *He sees the multitude in terms of individuals.*

To Him there are no masses; people are all unique human beings, each one in the sight of God more precious than the wealth of the whole world.

☐ *He treats people as needy without regard to position, wealth, or race.*

Since most people are poor, they receive the thrust of His ministry. Yet He does not ignore the rich and influential. Whatever the condition of men and women, everyone needs a shepherd. The gospel call is universal.

☐ *He responds to opportunities of ministry as they occur.*

Jesus has no office hours. He is always on the job. Anytime during the week, day or night, He stands ready to help. Wherever He happens to be—along the highway or seashore, desert or mountainside, home or business office, cemetery or synagogue—there He finds His pulpit and counseling room.

☐ *He utilizes the advantage of natural family relationships.*

His first contact is with a cousin. As to His brothers and sisters within the home of Joseph, their acceptance of His witness seems to be slow, but eventually (according to tradition) they follow their elder brother. Moreover, His primary ministry centers on Jews, people with whom He has a national and racial identity, though usually He does not hesitate to serve Gentiles when the occasion arises.

☐ *He notices signs of spiritual interest.*

Customarily, He attends religious services where seeking people are likely to gather. As He walks the streets, He looks for that longing soul at the seat of custom; He listens for the cry of the distressed over the noise of the crowd; He feels the touch of a feverish hand on His robe; He recognizes a little man gazing upon Him from the treetops. Sensitivity to such small matters often discovers persons desperate for God.

☐ *He seeks privacy with seekers where possible.*

Sometimes Jesus will take them aside from the multitude. Or He might disperse the crowd and deal with the person after the others are gone. Often He goes home with them, or they are invited to the place where He is staying. On a few occasions He meets one at a secluded spot where conversation is more relaxed. However arranged, getting away from distractions certainly facilitates better communication.

☐ *He takes time with people.*

Jesus can spend His lunch hour talking with a lonely woman, just as He can stay up late to visit with a member of the Sanhedrin. The rule seems to be that if a person is sincerely seeking help, He can find the time.

2. JESUS INSPIRES CONFIDENCE IN HIMSELF.

This is the appeal of His witness: He proves that He is a friend. People feel wanted and loved when they are with Him. When this comes through sincerely, we are assured a hearing.

☐ *He shows them that He cares.*

With divine insight, Jesus knows the feelings of the burdened and heavy-ladened, and He bids them come to Him. He is there when they are in physical crises. He weeps with them in their sorrow. He heals the sick and opens the eyes of the blind. He champions the cause of the widow and the orphan. Whatever the issue, He takes God's side against injustice and perversion. Though He does not attempt to overthrow the corrupt establishment of His day, he proclaims a Gospel that by its own power is destined to bring in a new order as men and women are changed within.

☐ *He observes common courtesies.*

Jesus is a gentleman. He addresses persons in authority by their proper titles. Except when cleansing the temple, He does not force Himself upon people uninvited. Nor does He forget to show appreciation to those who give Him hospitality. So important is sensitivity in these little things that once when the disciples forgot the customary washing of feet upon entering a house, Jesus sets an example before them by doing Himself this servant's duty.

☐ *He calls people by name.*

No sound is more familiar or appreciated by the ones addressed. His greetings convey a sense of warmth and dignity, creating a good first impression.

☐ *He commends persons for their good traits.*

His speech is not cheap flattery but the truth. Everyone has some admirable points. Even the arrogant lawyer is congratulated on his knowledge of the law, while the sinful woman of Samaria is reminded of her honesty in telling about her sin. Most people already know their shortcomings, but they may need help in finding their strengths.

☐ *He asks for small favors.*

Whether it is a drink of water, the use of a boat, or a place to spend the night, Jesus lets people help Him. Kept within the limits of propriety, the practice can be a way of making people feel needed.

☐ *He listens to their stories.*

People like to talk, especially about those things that are important to them. It takes patience to hear someone out, but it's a good way to help the person feel that you want to understand. And likely something will be learned about the reasons and forces, either real or imagined, that explain the life of the individual.

☐ *He interests Himself in their interests.*

Often this common concern, in turn, becomes the reference point for introducing a deeper message. Hence the water at the well becomes an illustration of living water and fishing an analogy of catching men. In this manner, He begins with the known and moves to the unknown—a fundamental rule in all teaching.

☐ *He communicates on their level.*

Jesus uses common, nontechnical language, full of local color. People can easily identify with His stories and figures of speech.

3. JESUS DRAWS OUT THEIR SPIRITUAL DESIRE.

Everyone has some inclination for God, for all persons are created in His image. This desire in some may seem very weak or completely suppressed, but it is still there. And until this spiritual nature is satisfied, no one can be at peace. Recognizing this fact and knowing the convicting power of the Holy Spirit, Jesus causes people to think deeply about their souls.

☐ *He assumes the best.*

Jesus acts as if people basically want true joy, peace, security, and eternal life. His attitude is invariably positive.

☐ *He asks probing questions.*

His queries usually center in the thing of immediate interest or curiosity and are not offensive. One question may follow another. Sometimes He interjects a question during a discourse to make sure that His thought is being followed. Or He might simply ask a rhetorical question to get the person's favorable response. The questions bring out the hidden problems and make people face the truth. They are also a means of directing the conversation without appearing dictatorial.

☐ *He states great spiritual propositions.*

Simple declarations often interpret an action or point out some basic principle. Used with discretion, forthright affirmations arrest attention and may cause one to ponder the truth deeply. If He is not understood the first time, Jesus might repeat the idea in a little different way to make sure that the lesson is not missed.

☐ *He projects the idea of God's blessing.*

He whets the aspirations of one's soul, making one hungry for what He has to offer. He likes to apply the spiritual benefit to the person's particular sore spot. Usually He speaks of the benefits of grace even as He makes evident the demands of repentance and faith. For example, by being born again, Nicodemus would "see the Kingdom of God." Whatever the cost of getting right, it cannot be compared with the glory to come.

☐ *He illustrates His ideas.*

Most common is the parable, whereby Jesus compares familiar facts with spiritual realities. In contrast to the fable, His stories deal with everyday situations that can be easily pictured. At times He may employ an object lesson, like the children, to exemplify His point. Or He might stimulate thought through some dramatic gesture, such as writing in the sand or touching the eyes of the blind.

☐ *He appeals to Scripture.*

To Him, the Old Testament is God's Word. He knows that what is written cannot be refuted. He likes to use this authority, especially when talking with persons who are well versed in the Bible. His favorite approach is to point out how the Scripture is fulfilled in present experience.

☐ *He shares His own testimony.*

It is always brief and to the point. There never is any doubt or confusion in His voice. With perfect assurance, He witnesses to that which He has seen and heard.

☐ *He refuses to argue.*

There are occasions when the scribes and Pharisees take exception to His teaching, and He corrects their perverted views. But even here His manner is more to affirm the truth and let the chips fall where they may.

4. JESUS CLARIFIES THE GOSPEL.

Desire is one thing, but really coming to grips with the meaning of salvation is another. The claims that Jesus makes upon us cannot be blurred. Until the message of God's grace is clear, one cannot make an intelligent choice. Yet being the perfect Teacher, He uses the highest type of teaching skill—the art that conceals art. The message is not obscured in the method.

☐ *He accents the essential truth of the kingdom.*

The good news is that the kingdom is present in Christ—He is the King—and we enter His kingdom now by faith through the Spirit of God. There is little effort to follow a systematic plan of salvation. Rather He gets across the idea crucial to that particular person. Every presentation is tailor-made for the occasion.

☐ *He uncovers sin.*

When the evil in us is ignored, Jesus does not hesitate to expose the condition. Sometimes He approaches the subject indirectly, as with the woman at the well. At other times, He comes to the point very bluntly, as with the Pharisees. But one way or another, the awful fact of human rebellion must be realized and the conscience awakened.

☐ *He reveals the grace of God.*

Here is the heart of the Gospel: nothing deserved; nothing earned. God simply gives Himself. He loves us in Christ when we are unloving. For the sake of His Son He saves "whosoever will" come to Him. The offer is fixed forever—sealed in blood. Since Jesus does it all, no work on our part is necessary. Indeed, we must confess our utter moral bankruptcy in order to receive His gift of salvation. Jesus makes clear that all we can do is believe.

☐ *He levels with people about the life of faith.*

Grace is free but not cheap. It cost God's Son His life, and it will mean the loss of ours if we take His teaching to heart. The cross permits no self-indulgence. Sin must be forsaken. Jesus offers no unrealistic bargains, as if by following Him all our problems will be solved. Quite the contrary. True discipleship is said to involve hardship, suffering, and persecution for righteousness' sake. What was mentioned in the beginning becomes increasingly obvious as the disciples walk with the Master.

☐ *He tests human motives.*

Just because one believes in a "sign" is no proof that the person believes in the Son. Nor is the desire to have some affliction healed or problem solved any indication of repentance. The greater the possibility that mere curiosity, awe, or selfish concern is the incentive, the greater the testing.

☐ *He personalizes the doctrine.*

Jesus does not ask anyone to embrace a creed or join an organization. Not that He opposes these things, but that the Gospel is finally disclosed in a Person—the incarnate Christ

Himself. Salvation is not a theological abstraction, but a living relationship with the Son of God.

☐ *He keeps to the subject.*

Again and again people try to get Jesus off on some tangent, which is not surprising in view of the foolish notions people can have, however sincere. Yet Jesus will not be diverted. Problems might be acknowledged, but then He politely brings the conversation back to the central issue.

☐ *He permits people to express back to Him their understanding of His teaching.*

By this procedure the person forms his or her own evaluation of the truth. It becomes apparent if correction or further elaboration is needed.

5. JESUS BRINGS PERSONS TO A DECISION.

Once the intellect is informed, He expects commitment. At this point the Gospel becomes decisive. One cannot remain neutral in the presence of Christ. His truth demands a verdict. Until there is consent to the will of God, people are lost.

☐ *He stresses individual responsibility.*

Greater privilege brings greater responsibility. Jesus speaks often of the judgment to come. Ultimately each person must give account.

☐ *He discloses the alternatives.*

A choice has to be made one way or the other. It is finally repent or perish, the narrow road or the broad way, abundant life or eternal death, heaven or hell.

☐ *He challenges people to exercise faith.*

The call is to action—"Arise," "Go," "Come down," "Enter," "Reach," "Sell what you have, give to the poor," "Take your cross and come, follow Me." By doing something, the person demonstrates trust. Faith is taken out of the realm of theory. Jesus does not ask for professions, but obedience to His Word.

☐ *He lets persons express their confidence in the most realistic way.*

To the lame, it is to walk; to the weeping woman, it is to stop crying and go in peace; to the scribe, it is to keep the law. The prescription, like the examination, is suited to the person.

☐ *He encourages the fainthearted.*

"Arise, be not afraid," "Son, be of good cheer." Such words, coupled with His compassionate deeds, give a gentle nudge to make that first trembling move toward God.

☐ *He respects their freedom.*

There is no example of Jesus ever chiding or forcing persons against their will. He does all He can to make the issue plain and bring response, but the decision rests with the individual.

☐ *He waits on the Spirit.*

Jesus knows that the harvest takes time. The seed planted needs to germinate and grow. He can be patient, for He realizes that God is working even when there is no visible evidence of change. The precise moment, mode, and place of decision is not of major consequence. What matters is the conscious set of the heart to go with God.

☐ *He rejoices in the victory.*

With the angels that celebrate over one sinner that repents, Jesus found great satisfaction in the knowledge that His kingdom was coming. Ultimately His church would storm the gates of hell. Whatever hindrances were encountered along the way, He knew that at last the Gospel would be preached in all the world for a witness and that the Son of Man would reign over a kingdom of the born again gathered from every tongue and tribe and nation.

6. JESUS NURTURES BELIEVERS IN HIS LIFE.

Follow-up is the key to His evangelism. Commitment to Him is the beginning of a continuing relationship objectified in the church. Yet a person must have a helping hand until he or she is able to bring others to life.

☐ *He stays with believers as time allows.*

This is the secret of His approach with new converts. They are together as much as possible—at home, along the road, in the synagogue. When they get separated, He finds them again. Certainly the best way to give guidance is through personal contact.

☐ *He explains more about life in the Spirit.*

Most people need a lot of help in understanding the theology of conversion, to say nothing of growth in the Christian life. The question again is an important tool in His approach: "What," "Why," and "How." Also, Jesus is there to respond to *their* questions. His instruction usually is precipitated by some immediate circumstance. Teaching situations that arise in such a setting are always more convincing.

☐ *He stimulates witness.*

The redeemed of the Lord should not be ashamed to express their thanksgiving. Jesus often reminds us of the obligation to tell what great things God has done. The few times when He requests persons not to broadcast a miracle seem to be in deference to the excitability of the crowd, and are not the rule.

☐ *He builds the Word into their lives.*

The Scriptures are the written authority for their faith. Believers cannot survive long without it, nor can they go on in the deeper things of God. This is even more crucial after Jesus ascends to heaven. But while He is with them, He constantly refers them to the Bible and applies its wisdom to their need.

☐ *He teaches people to pray.*

The practice of this devotion in His own life is observed by His followers, and before long they are asking to learn His secret. The first lesson is very simple. He just puts the words in their mouths. But soon they are able to pray on their own. Progressively He teaches them more about communion and depending upon God for a daily supply of grace.

☐ *He surrounds His people with a fellowship of love.*

No one can come to Jesus and remain alone. Every believer becomes a part of a company of faith. This is visibly experienced in the group that follows Him and in the little clusters of the faithful wherever He goes. Their usual meeting place is in a home, yet they are not bound by any building.

☐ *He prepares them to face temptations in the world.*

Though His followers are told to sin no more, there is no illusion about the evil environment in which they live. Jesus warns them of the dangers and teaches them to resist the beguiling attacks of Satan.

☐ *He brings believers into His ministry.*

To follow Jesus means that one becomes involved in what He is doing. According to ability, everyone can do something—provide a house, cook, contribute money, assist in baptism and healing, visit, teach, and in many other ways contribute to His work. There is a place for everyone in the work of Christ.

7. JESUS EXPECTS DISCIPLES TO REPRODUCE.

Thus the cycle begins anew. The process of winning persons is completed only when its continuation is assured. This is the genius of His evangelism. As churches reproduce their kind through the Holy Spirit and teach those they win to reach others, eventually the world will be reached with the Gospel.

Here all of us are brought to evaluate our own ministry. Are we reproducing our lives in others? Are we training them for the harvest?

Hopefully this study has helped reinforce these priorities while also providing some guidelines for personal evangelism. Much more needs to be explored and applied, but at least the basic direction has been charted. It remains for us now to translate our insights into daily life.

The legend is told that when Jesus returned to heaven, He was asked by the angel Gabriel what plans he had made to carry on His work. "Well, I have given the Gospel to Peter and Mary and the other disciples," He said. "They will tell others."

"But suppose Peter gets too busy with his fishing and Mary too occupied with her housework and the others too concerned with their business, and they forget to pass the word along," the angel replied. "What plans have you then to reach the world with the good news?"

There was a momentary pause. Then with confidence in His voice, Jesus turned to Gabriel and said, "I have no other plans. I am counting on them!"

Amazing as it may seem, that is the plan. Can He count on you?

NOTES

Introduction

1. This concept and its implementation is discussed in my book *The Master Plan of Evangelism* (Old Tappan, N.J.: Fleming H. Revell, 1963, 1964, 1993). Since it deals with the basic philosophy of Jesus' evangelism and His long-term planning, the book should be read in preparation for this study. A study guide by Dr. Roy J. Fish is included in the newest edition of the book.

2. The apostle Paul mentions that Jesus appeared to about five hundred believers after His resurrection, most of whom were still living at the time he wrote the Corinthian letter (1 Corinthians 15:6).

One: First Disciples

1. Only the account in Luke tells about preaching to the crowd. Because Mark and Matthew omit this detail, there may seem to be a discrepancy between their narratives and that of the more complete story. The problem is resolved when Luke 5:1-4 is seen as an elaboration of Mark 1:16 and Matthew 4:18. Subsequent events may be arranged by comparing the details that follow in the three descriptions.

Three: Sinful Women

1. This account probably was not part of the original gospel of John, but it is still regarded as a true story. Most New Testament authorities believe it was taken from the collection of Papias during the middle of the second century.

Five: Proud and Contrite

1. This anointing is not to be confused with the later episode at Bethany six days before his death (Matthew 26:6). Though there are similarities in the two accounts, the differences make any identification unlikely. Here Simon is a Pharisee; in the other he is a "leper." Here the people at the feast seem unsympathetic toward Jesus; in the other he is among friends. Here anointing is an expression of love resulting from forgiveness; in the other it is in anticipation of His burial. Some authorities have associated the woman in the story with Mary of Magdala. However, this is pure conjecture. Mary Magdalene is mentioned in the next chapter (Luke 8:2), but in connection with a different setting.

Seven: The Blind

1. Matthew mentions two blind men, while Mark and Luke describe only the conspicuous one. The indication that the healing took place as Jesus went out from Jericho, noted by Matthew, probably refers to leaving the old city, whereas Mark and Luke speak of Jesus approaching the new city built by Herod the Great.

Eight: Vicarious Believers

1. Matthew's version says that the centurion came himself, while Luke's record indicates he sent elders. What might appear to be a discrepancy is resolved when it is understood that a delegation can speak for the one authorizing the mission. In this case, Matthew, following accepted custom, merely alludes to the one dispatching the authorized spokesman, while Luke gives the particulars.

Ten: Demoniacs

1. Matthew says there were two demoniacs; Mark and Luke describe only one, who was probably the most prominent.

Twelve: Chief of Sinners

1. The form in which Christ appears to Saul in the blinding light is not explained. Of this we are sure—He is the same Person who

died on the cross and rose again, and the voice is the same that had spoken in Jesus of Nazareth. The first account is told by the historian Luke; the other two are records of Paul's own narration. No single record gives all the details, but by comparing the three, it is possible to see a fairly clear sequence.

BIBLIOGRAPHY

B ooks that bear upon the evangelism of Jesus are plentiful and generally accessible. In this vast collection are commentaries, histories of the period, stories of the life and teaching of Christ, accounts of His disciples, and some works especially treating the way He confronted people with the Gospel. The volumes selected here should be considered only as an introduction to the subject. Added to the list of biblical studies are some practical how-to books on personal evangelism. The student will find titles marked with an asterisk a good place to begin a reading program.

The Life and Times of Christ

Berkouwer, G. C. *The Person of Christ.* Grand Rapids: Wm. B. Eerdmans, 1954.

Bonsirven, Joseph. *Palestinian Judaism in the Time of Jesus Christ.* New York: Holt, Rinehart and Winston, 1964.

Braun, Herbert. *Jesus of Nazareth: the Man and His Time.* Philadelphia: Fortress, 1979.

Bruce, F. F. *Jesus, Lord and Savior.* Downers Grove, Ill.: InterVarsity, 1986.

Burridge, Richard A. *Four Gospels, One Jesus?* Grand Rapids: Wm. B. Eerdmans, 1994.

Edersheim, Alfred. *The Life and Times of Jesus the Messiah.* Updated ed. Peabody, Mass.: Hendrickson, 1883, 1993.

Farrar, Frederic W. *The Life of Christ.* Portland, Ore.: Fountain, 1874, 1964.

Gire, Ken. *Incredible Moments with the Savior.* Grand Rapids: Zondervan, 1990.

Green, Joel B. and Scott McKnight, eds. *Dictionary of Jesus and the Gospels.* Downers Grove, Ill.: InterVarsity, 1992.

*Guthrie, Donald. *Jesus the Messiah.* Grand Rapids: Zondervan, 1972.

_____. *A Shorter Life of Christ.* Grand Rapids: Zondervan, 1970.

Harrison, Everett F. *A Short Life of Christ.* Grand Rapids: Wm. B. Eerdmans, 1968.

Hobbs, Herschel H. *The Life and Times of Jesus.* Grand Rapids: Zondervan, 1966.

Jeremias, Joachum. *Jerusalem in the Time of Jesus.* Philadelphia: Fortress, 1969.

Lange, J. P. *The Life of the Lord Jesus Christ.* 4 vols. Grand Rapids: Zondervan, 1872, 1958.

Letham, Robert. *The Work of Christ.* Downers Grove, Ill.: InterVarsity, 1993.

Marshall, I. Howard. *The Work of Christ.* Grand Rapids: Zondervan, 1969, 1970.

Metzger, Bruce. *The New Testament: Its Background, Growth, and Content.* New York: Abingdon, 1965.

Oden, Thomas C. *The Word of Life.* Systematic Theology, vol. 2. New York: Harper & Row, 1989.

Oursler, Fulton. *The Greatest Story Ever Told.* New York: Doubleday, 1949, 1953.

Robertson, A. T. *Epochs in the Life of Jesus.* New York: Scribners, 1920.

Sheen, Fulton J. *Life of Christ.* New York: McGraw-Hill, 1958.

Smith, David. *The Days of His Flesh.* London: Hodder and Stoughton, 1910.

Stalker, James. *The Life of Jesus Christ.* Grand Rapids: Zondervan, 1889, 1983.

Tenney, Merrill C. *New Testament Times.* Grand Rapids: Wm. B. Eerdmans, 1965.

Thiede, Carsten Peter and Matthew D'Ancona. *Eyewitnesses to Jesus.* New York: Doubleday, 1996.

Vollmer, Philip. *The Modern Student's Life of Christ.* New York: Fleming H. Revell, 1912.

Witherington, Ben. *The Jesus Quest.* Downers Grove, Ill.: InterVarsity, 1995.

The Thought of Jesus

Beasley-Murray, George R. *Jesus and the Last Days.* Peabody, Mass.: Hendrickson, 1993.

Boice, James M. *The Sermon on the Mount.* Grand Rapids: Zondervan, 1972.

Capon, Robert Farrar. *The Parables of the Kingdom.* Grand Rapids: Wm. B. Eerdmans, 1988.

Carson, D. A. *The Sermon on the Mount.* Grand Rapids: Baker, 1978.

*Coleman, Robert E. *The Mind of the Master*. With Study Guide. Old Tappan, N.J.: Fleming H. Revell, 1977.

_____. *The Great Communion Lifestyle*. Grand Rapids: Baker/Fleming H. Revell, 1992.

Crane, Louis Burton. *The Teaching of Jesus Concerning the Holy Spirit*. New York: American Tract Society, 1905.

France, R. T. *Jesus and the Old Testament*. London: Tyndale, 1971.

Henry, Carl F. H. *The Identity of Jesus of Nazareth*. Nashville: Broadman, 1992.

Hunter, A. M. *The Work and Words of Jesus*. Rev. ed. London: SCM Press, 1950, 1973.

Kistemaker, Simon J. *The Parables of Jesus*. Grand Rapids: Baker, 1980.

Ladd, G. E. *The Presence of the Future*. Grand Rapids: Wm. B. Eerdmans, 1974.

Lloyd-Jones, D. Martyn. *Studies in the Sermon on the Mount*. 2 vols. London: InterVarsity, 1959, 1960.

Lockyer, Herbert. *All the Teachings of Jesus*. San Francisco: Harper, 1991.

Manson, Thomas Walter. *The Teachings of Jesus*. Cambridge: Cambridge University, 1931, 1963.

Morgan, G. Campbell. *The Teaching of Christ*. New York: Fleming H. Revell, 1913.

Murray, Andrew. *Like Christ*. Minneapolis: Bethany Fellowship, 1974.

_____. *The Spirit of Christ*. Fort Washington, Penn.: Christian Literature Crusade, 1888, 1970.

_____. *With Christ in the School of Prayer*. Grand Rapids: Zondervan, 1885, 1983.

Neil, William. *The Difficult Sayings of Jesus*. Grand Rapids: Wm. B. Eerdmans, 1975.

Pentecost, J. Dwight. *Design for Living.* Chicago: Moody, 1975.

Pink, Arthur W. *An Exposition of the Sermon on the Mount.* Grand Rapids: Baker, 1958.

Stewart, James. *The Life and Teaching of Jesus.* Nashville: Abingdon, 1957.

Studdert-Kennedy, G. A. *The Wicket Gate.* London: Hodder and Stoughton, 1923.

Stott, John. *Christ the Controversialist.* Downers Grove, Ill.: InterVarsity, 1970.

Trench, R. C. *Notes on the Parable of Our Lord.* Grand Rapids: Baker, 1948, 1977.

Wenham, J. W. *Christ and the Bible.* Grand Rapids: Baker, 1972, 1994.

Jesus and His Disciples

Barclay, William. *The Master's Men.* London: SCM Press, 1959.

Brown, Charles R. *The Twelve.* New York: Harper, 1926.

Bruce, A. B. *The Training of the Twelve.* Grand Rapids: Kregel, 1871, 1970.

*Coleman, Robert E. *The Master Plan of Evangelism.* With Study Guide by Roy Fish, rev. 30th anniversary ed. Grand Rapids: Revell/Baker, 1963, 1964, 1993.

_____. *The Master Plan of Discipleship.* Old Tappan, N.J.: Fleming H. Revell, 1987.

Doraisamy, Theodore R. *Jesus and His Disciples.* Singapore: Methodist Book Room, 1988.

Flynn, Leslie B. *The Twelve.* Wheaton, Ill.: Victor, 1982.

Ford, Leighton. *Transforming Leadership.* Downers Grove, Ill.: InterVarsity, 1991.

George, Edward Augustua. *The Twelve.* New York: Fleming H. Revell, 1916.

Glover, Carl A. *With the Twelve.* Nashville: Cokesbury, 1939.

Hull, Bill. *Jesus Christ: Disciple Maker.* Grand Rapids: Baker, 1990.

Kraus, C. Norman. *Jesus Christ Our Lord: Christology from a Disciple's Perspective.* Scottdale: Herald Press, 1987.

LaSor, William Sanford. *Great Personalities of the New Testament.* Westwood, N.J.: Fleming H. Revell, 1971.

Latham, Henry. *Pastor Pastorium.* Cambridge: Deighton Bell, 1910.

Mackay, W. Mackintosh. *The Men Whom Jesus Made.* New York: George H. Doran, 1924.

Meye, Robert P. *Jesus and the Twelve.* Grand Rapids: Wm. B. Eerdmans, 1968.

Morton, T. Ralph. *The Twelve Together.* Glasgow: The Ione Community, 1956.

Palmer, F. Noel. *Christ's Way with People.* London: Marshall, Morgan & Scott, 1943.

Robinson, Benjamin W. *Jesus in Action.* New York: Macmillan, 1942.

Schell, Edwin. *Traits of the Twelve.* Cincinnati: Jennings and Graham, 1911.

Smith, Asbury. *The Twelve Christ Chose.* New York: Harper, 1958.

Strong, Kendrick. *All the Master's Men.* Chappaqua, N.Y.: Christian Herald Books, 1978.

Ward, J. W. G. *The Master and the Twelve.* New York: George H. Doran, 1924.

Wilson, Carl. *With Christ in the School of Disciple Building.* Grand Rapids: Zondervan, 1976.

Wilkins, Michael J. *Following the Master: Discipleship in the Steps of Jesus*. Grand Rapids: Zondervan, 1992.

Witherspoon, Francis. *The Glorious Company*. New York: Harcourt, Brace, 1928.

The Teaching Method of Jesus

Beardslee, C. S. *Teacher Training with the Master Teacher*. Philadelphia: The Sunday School Times, 1903.

Bruce, A. B. *The Parabolic Teaching of Christ*. New York: A. C. Armstrong & Son, 1908.

Crawford, Clarence W. *Taught by the Master*. Nashville: Broadman, 1956.

Curtis, W. A. *Jesus Christ the Teacher*. London: Oxford University, 1943.

Delnay, Robert G. *Teach as He Taught*. Chicago: Moody, 1987.

Gregory, Milton. *The Seven Laws of Teaching*. Grand Rapids: Baker, 1886, 1971.

Hendricks, Howard G. *Teaching to Change Lives*. Portland, Ore.: Multnomah, 1987.

*Horne, Herman H. *Teaching Techniques of Jesus (Jesus the Master Teacher)*. Grand Rapids: Kregel, 1920, 1971.

Jones, Claude C. *The Teaching Methods of the Master*. St. Louis: Bethany, 1957.

Marquis, John A. *Learning to Teach from the Master Teacher*. Philadelphia: Westminster, 1918.

McCoy, C. F. *The Art of Jesus as a Teacher*. Philadelphia: Judson, 1930.

Perkins, Pheme. *Jesus as Teacher*. Cambridge, England: Cambridge University Press, 1990.

Price, J. M. *Jesus the Teacher*. Nashville: Convention, 1954.

Raven, Charles E. Christ and Modern Education. New York: Henry Holt, 1928.

Richardson, Norman E. *The Christ of the Classroom*. New York: Macmillan, 1931.

Sharman, H. H. *Jesus as Teacher*. New York: Harper, 1935.

Squire, Walter Albion. *The Pedagogy of Jesus*. Philadelphia: Westminster, 1927.

Updike, Paul. *As Jesus Taught Them*. Kansas City: Beacon Hill, 1947.

Personal Interviews of Jesus

Barker, William P. *Personalities Around Jesus*. Old Tappan, N.J.: Fleming H. Revell, 1968.

Calkins, Raymond. *How Jesus Dealt with Man*. Nashville: Abingdon-Cokesbury, 1939.

Cornell, George W. *They Knew Jesus*. New York: William Morrow and Company, 1957.

Duncan, B. H. *Personal Adventures with Jesus*. Nashville: Broadman, 1949.

Ford, Leighton. *Meeting Jesus*. Downers Grove, Ill.: InterVarsity, 1988.

Hunter, John. *Impact*. Glendale: Regal, 1966.

MacCartney, C. E. *Great Interviews with Jesus*. New York: Abingdon, 1944.

McConaughy, James. *Christ Among Man*. Newark: International Committee of YMCA, 1902.

McFatridge, F. V. *The Personal Evangelism of Jesus*. Grand Rapids: Zondervan, 1939.

*Morgan, G. Campbell. *The Great Physician*. Old Tappan, N.J.:
Fleming H. Revell, 1937, 1972.

Rolston, Holmes. *Faces About the Cross*. Richmond: John Knox,
1959.

Scarborough, L. F. *How Jesus Won Men*. New York: George H.
Doran, 1926.

Sligh, John. *Christ's Way of Winning Souls*. Nashville: Publishing
House of the M. E. Church, South, 1909.

Smart, James D. *The Quiet Revolution*. Philadelphia: Westminster,
1969.

Smith, John. *The Magnetism of Christ*. London: Hodder and
Stoughton, 1904.

Stokes, Mack. *The Evangelism of Jesus*. Nashville: Methodist
Evangelistic Materials, 1960.

Walker, Alan. *How Jesus Helped People*. New York: Abingdon,
1964.

Wareing, Earnest Clyde. *The Evangelism of Jesus*. New York:
Abingdon, 1918.

Whitesell, Faris D. *Basic New Testament Evangelism*. Grand
Rapids: Zondervan, 1949.

Contemporary Methods of Personal Evangelism and Discipleship

Aldrich, Joseph. *Gentle Persuasion*. Portland, Ore.: Multnomah,
1990.

Barna, George. *Evangelism That Works*. Ventura, Calif.: Regal,
1995.

Beougher, Sharon and Mary Dorsett. *Women and Evangelism: An
Evangelistic Lifestyle from a Woman's Perspective*. Wheaton,
Ill.: Billy Graham Center IOE, 1994.

Bright, Bill. *Witnessing Without Fear.* San Bernardino, Calif.: Here's Life Publishers, 1987.

Coleman, Robert E., with Timothy Beougher and Tom Phillips, eds. *Disciplemaking: A Self-Study Course on Follow-Up and Discipleship.* Wheaton, Ill.: Billy Graham Center IOE, 1994.

Coppedge, Allan. *The Biblical Principles of Discipleship.* Grand Rapids: Francis Asbury/Zondervan, 1989.

Eims, Leroy. *The Lost Art of Disciple Making.* Grand Rapids: Zondervan, 1978.

Fish, Roy J. and J. E. Conant. *Every Member Evangelism for Today.* New York: Harper & Row, 1922, 1976.

Ford, Kevin Graham. *Jesus for a New Generation.* Downers Grove, Ill.: InterVarsity, 1995.

Ford, Leighton. *The Power of Story.* Colorado Springs: NavPress, 1994.

*Heck, Joel D., ed. *The Art of Sharing Your Faith.* Old Tappan, N.J.: Fleming H. Revell, 1991.

Hendricks, Howard G. *Say It with Love.* Wheaton, Ill.: Victor, 1972.

Hendrickson, Walter A. *Disciples Are Made—Not Born.* Wheaton, Ill.: Victor, 1975.

Hybels, Bill and Mark Mettleberg. *Becoming a Contagious Christian.* Grand Rapids: Zondervan, 1994.

Kennedy, James. *Evangelism Explosion.* 3rd. ed. Wheaton, Ill.: Tyndale, 1983.

Kramp, John. *Out of Their Faces and into Their Shoes.* Nashville: Broadman, 1995.

Little, Paul. *How to Give Away Your Faith.* Downers Grove, Ill.: InterVarsity, 1966.

McCloskey, Mark. *Tell It Often—Tell It Well.* Pasadena: Here's Life Publishers, 1986.

Moore, Waylon. *New Testament Follow-Up for Pastors and Laymen.* Grand Rapids: Wm. B. Eerdmans, 1972.

Neighbor, Ralph. *Where Do We Go from Here.* Houston: Torch, 1990.

Olford, Steven F. *The Secret of Soul-Winning.* Chicago: Moody, 1963.

Parish, Archie and John. *Best Friends.* Nashville: Oliver/Nelson, 1984, 1986.

Phillips, Keith. *The Making of a Disciple.* Old Tappan, N.J.: Fleming H. Revell, 1981.

Poterski, Donald C. *Reinventing Evangelism.* Downers Grove, Ill.: InterVarsity, 1989.

Rainer, Thom S., ed. *Evangelism in the Twenty-First Century.* Wheaton, Ill.: Harold Shaw, 1989.

Robinson, Bill D. *Getting Beyond the Small Talk.* Minneapolis: Worldwide, 1989.

Robinson, Darnell. *People Sharing Jesus.* Nashville: Thomas Nelson, 1995.

Schweer, G. William. *Personal Evangelism for Today.* Nashville: Broadman, 1984.

Shaver, Charles "Chuck." *The Bible Speaks to Me About My Witness.* Kansas City: Beacon Hill, 1991.

Spurgeon, Charles H. *The Soul Winner.* David Otis Fuller, ed. Grand Rapids: Zondervan, 1948.

Strobel, Lee. *Inside the Mind of Unchurched Harry and Mary.* Grand Rapids: Zondervan, 1993.

Tam, Stanley. *Every Christian a Soul-Winner.* Nashville: Thomas Nelson, 1975.

Thompson, W. Oscar, Jr. *Concentric Circles of Concern.* Nashville: Broadman, 1981.

Towns, Elmer, ed. *A Practical Encyclopedia: Evangelism and Church Growth.* Ventura, Calif.: Regal, 1996.

Trotman, Dawson. *Born to Reproduce.* Lincoln, Neb.: Back to the Bible, 1964.

Warr, Gene. *You Can Make Disciples.* Waco, Tex.: Word, 1978.

Wiles, Jerry. *How to Win Others to Christ.* Nashville: Thomas Nelson, 1992.